Contents

"The Linux philosophy is 'Laugh in the face of danger'. Oops. Wrong One. 'Do it yourself'. Yes, that's it."

— Linus Torvalds

1. Introduction to the World of Linux Linking

Welcome to "Linking with the Linker: Playing with Linux Libraries," a comprehensive guide designed not only for seasoned developers but also for those taking their first steps into the vast and rich ecosystem of Linux. In this book, we journey into the intricate realm of dynamic and static libraries, demystifying the processes that underpin the highly efficient operations within Linux environments. Although the world of linking can appear daunting, this guide aims to present it in a straightforward, approachable manner, offering insights and practical examples every step of the way. Whether you're an enthusiastic programmer seeking more control over your applications or a dedicated system administrator eager to understand how linking affects system performance, this guide is tailored for you. Together, we will explore the architectures and mechanisms of linking, empowering you to leverage your understanding of Linux libraries like never before.

2. Understanding Linux Libraries

2.1. What is a Library?

Libraries in the context of software development serve as vital repositories of code that developers utilize to streamline their workflow and enhance the capabilities of their applications. A library, in technical terms, is a collection of precompiled routines that a program can use. These routines, referred to as functions or methods, can be invoked in the program without the developer needing to understand their underlying code. This abstraction not only expedites the coding process but also paves the way for reusability and modularity within applications.

The significance of libraries is especially pronounced in the Linux ecosystem, where they facilitate a wide range of tasks and functionalities across various domains, including system programming, application development, and web services. By consolidating common tasks into easily accessible libraries, developers save valuable time – coding once and reusing that code across multiple projects without the need to repeatedly implement standard functions. This also leads to more efficient use of resources and significantly reduces the chances of introducing bugs, as established libraries undergo thorough testing and refinement.

From a practical standpoint, libraries can be divided into two main categories: static and dynamic libraries. Static libraries, often denoted by a .a extension, are linked into the application at compile time, becoming a part of the final executable. Conversely, dynamic libraries, indicated by the .so extension in Linux, are linked at runtime, allowing multiple programs to share the same library code, which saves memory and disk space while promoting efficiency in updates and maintenance.

Dynamic libraries also offer a significant advantage in terms of version management. When a library is updated, all applications utilizing that library can benefit from the improvements or bug fixes without requiring recompilation. This flexibility is crucial in environments where software must remain operational without extended downtime for updates, making dynamic libraries particularly appealing for web servers and large-scale applications.

Moreover, the importance of libraries extends into the realms of security and optimization. By leveraging established libraries, developers can reduce exposure to potential security vulnerabilities that may arise from homegrown code. Well-maintained libraries receive attention from the community and are regularly updated to address newly discovered vulnerabilities, thus providing an additional layer of security.

In addition to enhancing security, libraries contribute to performance optimization. Functions within libraries can be thoroughly vetted and optimized, ensuring they run efficiently. Developers can thus tap into this optimized code, benefiting from performance enhancements that might be difficult to achieve in isolated projects. This leads to applications that not only perform better but also consume fewer resources, which is especially vital in resource-constrained environments.

Furthermore, libraries foster collaboration and innovation. In the Linux community, for example, numerous open-source libraries are available for developers to use, adapt, and improve upon. This communal approach to code sharing catalyzes innovation, as developers can build upon each other's work, creating more sophisticated systems and applications that advance the capabilities of the technology as a whole.

Despite these advantages, it is essential to note that incorporating libraries into applications comes with its challenges. Dependencies may lead to conflicts when differing libraries require different versions of the same components. Additionally, reliance on third-party libraries means that developers must remain vigilant about the status of those libraries, ensuring they are regularly updated and secure. Proper dependency management becomes crucial, particularly in large projects where numerous libraries interact.

In summary, libraries are an indispensable component of software development, enabling developers to build robust, efficient, and maintainable applications. They streamline the coding process by providing reusable code, enhance performance and security, and foster collaboration and innovation within the community. As the Linux ecosystem continues to evolve, libraries will remain a cornerstone of software development, underpinning applications that are not only functional but also aligned with best practices in efficiency, security, and performance. Understanding the nature and role of libraries is thus fundamental for anyone traversing the landscape of Linux application development.

2.2. The Types of Libraries

Libraries are fundamental components in the architecture of modern software development, particularly within the Linux ecosystem, and they come in various forms that serve different purposes. At the heart of the understanding of libraries lies the categorization into static and dynamic libraries, each with its unique characteristics, advantages, and use cases.

Static libraries, identifiable by their file extensions typically ending in .a, are archives of object files. These libraries are linked into executables at compile time, effectively merging the library code with the application code, resulting in a single executable file. This means that all the necessary code from the statically linked library is included within the final binary. Consequently, when the application runs, it has all dependencies packaged, which can greatly enhance the performance and speed of the application in scenarios where rapid execution is vital. However, there are trade-offs to this approach. The increased size of executables is a significant downside, which can lead to higher storage requirements and potentially longer load times. Furthermore, if a static library is updated, it necessitates recompiling any dependent applications to take advantage of improvements or fixes.

On the other hand, dynamic libraries, designated with the .so extension in Linux (shared objects), are linked during runtime rather than compile time. This enables multiple applications to use the same library code simultaneously without duplicating it in each executable file. Consequently, the system benefits from reduced memory usage since shared libraries are loaded only once into memory, regardless of how many applications are using them. Dynamic libraries also enhance maintainability; changing a library (updating for bug fixes or performance enhancements) does not require any modifications to the executable files that depend on it. A significant benefit here is the flexibility afforded to system administrators and developers, as they can update libraries independently of the applications that utilize them, leading to reduced downtime and a more seamless user experience.

The choice between static and dynamic libraries often involves a careful evaluation of a project's requirements. Static linking can offer performance advantages in scenarios where execution speed is paramount, such as in embedded systems or applications where minimizing load times directly impacts user experience. Conversely, dynamic libraries shine in environments that require frequent updates and maintenance since they simplify the process of deploying fixes or enhancements across multiple applications. Developers also often face considerations regarding licensing and compatibility when choosing libraries; ensuring consistent library versions and maintaining compatibility with existing codebases can be crucial for long-term project sustainability.

Moreover, libraries can also be classified based on their functionality and purpose beyond just static and dynamic distinctions. For instance, there are system libraries, which provide critical system-level functionality and are usually part of the operating system; user libraries, which encapsulate features meant for direct use by applications; and third-party libraries, which are usually open-source or proprietary software solutions that developers can leverage to introduce advanced functionalities without having to build them from scratch.

In addition to these classifications, the development community has invented countless libraries that target specific domains or requirements, from graphics rendering to database management. For example, libraries such as GTK and Qt offer frameworks for building graphical user interfaces, while libraries such as OpenSSL provide vital cryptography functions necessary for secure applications. The variety and specialization of libraries empower developers to focus on building unique features for their applications, optimizing the time spent on generic tasks.

Ultimately, the landscape of libraries within Linux is both diverse and evolving, offering a wealth of choices for developers and system architects to navigate. Understanding the types of libraries, their characteristics, and when to utilize each type is crucial for leveraging their full potential. The symbiotic relationship between static and dynamic libraries presents opportunities for building efficient, flexible, and maintainable applications, aligning with best practices in modern software development while paving the way for innovation and creativity in coding practices. As Linux continues to evolve, the emphases on modularity, efficiency, and sustainability in library management will remain at the forefront of effective software design.

2.3. Why Use Libraries?

In the landscape of software development, libraries stand out as powerful enablers of efficiency, scalability, and quality. Their use in programming, particularly within the Linux environment, offers a multitude of advantages that are not only foundational but transformative for developers across varying skill levels and project scales. One of the most significant benefits of utilizing libraries is code reuse. By leveraging pre-existing libraries, developers can avoid the need to write common functionality from scratch. This practice not only accelerates the development process but also fosters greater consistency across projects, as libraries often encapsulate best practices that have been refined through community feedback and use over time.

Efficiency is another paramount reason for using libraries. Reducing the volume of code that developers need to maintain leads to less complexity and a decrease in the potential for bugs. For instance, a well-maintained library like the GNU C Library (glibc) has been subjected to extensive testing across various scenarios. Thus, developers can trust its reliability rather than recreating complex routines themselves, which may inadvertently introduce errors. The efficiencies gained through libraries can ultimately translate into performance improvements for the end user. As libraries are often optimized for specific tasks, developers who utilize them can build applications that run faster and more efficiently than those coded entirely from scratch.

Maintenance becomes significantly simpler with the use of libraries as well. When a bug is identified or a feature needs enhancement within a library, developers make updates in one central location. This centralized approach contrasts sharply with modifying and redeploying code across multiple applications, which can be error-prone and time-consuming. By employing dynamic libraries in particular, software developers can update applications without requiring recompilation of the entire system. This is especially beneficial in production environments where downtime must be minimized.

Moreover, libraries encourage modularity in software design. A modular approach not only enhances code organization but also makes systems easier to maintain and expand. With modular libraries, developers can build applications that are not only interoperable with existing systems but are also adaptable to future needs. This adaptability is particularly important as technology and requirements evolve rapidly. Developers can seamlessly integrate new libraries or swap out existing ones to add functionality or improve performance, ensuring their applications remain relevant and efficient.

The use of libraries also promotes collaboration within the development community. Many Linux libraries are open source, which means they are available for anyone to use, modify, and improve upon. This collaborative spirit fosters innovation, as developers can contribute enhancements, report issues, or create complementary tools. Such community-driven efforts often lead to libraries that are more robust and feature-rich than those that could be developed by a single entity or organization. Additionally, shared libraries serve a dual purpose by allowing different applications to use the same underlying code. This not only reduces duplication of effort but also means a single update to a library benefits all applications that rely on it.

While the advantages of using libraries are substantial, they come with certain responsibilities and considerations. As developers integrate third-party libraries into their projects, they must pay attention to licensing agreements to ensure compliance with legal parameters. Furthermore, dependency management becomes crucial, particularly in large projects where conflicts may arise from different versions of the same library. This necessitates a thorough understanding of the libraries being used, their update cycles, and the implications of any changes made, ensuring a balance between leveraging community resources and maintaining control over one's own codebase.

In conclusion, the rationale for using libraries within Linux software development cannot be overstated. They provide a compelling mix of code reuse, efficiency, ease of maintenance, modular design, and collaborative opportunity. As applications become increasingly complex, the role of libraries in managing that complexity becomes all the more critical. The correct use of libraries not only smooths the development process but also leads to stronger, more resilient software solutions. With the fast-paced evolution of technology, understanding the importance and utility of libraries is integral for any developer aiming to thrive in the Linux ecosystem. Libraries are not just tools—they are the building blocks that facilitate innovation, robust performance, and simplified code management in modern software development.

2.4. The Role of the Linker

The linker serves as a crucial intermediary in the software development process, enabling the integration of code and facilitating the creation of executable files that run smoothly on Linux systems. At its core, the linker's primary function is to take one or more object files generated by a compiler and combine them into a single executable file, a shared library, or another object file. While this may seem straightforward, the complexities of this process are significant; understanding them unveils the pivotal role linkers play in the broader context of Linux development.

When a programmer writes code in a high-level programming language, that code is first translated into object code, which is machine-readable, by a compiler. However, this compilation often results in multiple object files, especially in larger projects that are organized into distinct modules for maintainability and clarity. Each object file represents a specific part of the program—the functions, variables, and data structures defined within. The linker is responsible for merging these object files together, resolving references to shared symbols across them, and ensuring that when the program runs, all pieces of code and data are accessible and correctly located in memory.

One of the primary roles of the linker is to resolve symbols, which are essentially names that represent functions or variables in the code. For example, if one object file calls a function defined in another file, the linker ensures that it finds the correct address of that function. This involves not only bringing together various object files but also linking to relevant libraries that contain precompiled functions and routines that the programmer might have employed throughout the code.

Linkers perform critical tasks, including symbol resolution, relocation, and addressing. Symbol resolution involves determining the proper addresses for functions and variables; relocation adjusts the addresses in the object files so that they correctly point to the locations in memory where the final executable will reside. These processes are vital for constructing applications that run effectively and reliably.

In Linux, linkers also handle the inclusion of dynamic libraries at runtime, which adds another layer of complexity to their role. The dynamic linker, specifically, manages shared libraries that can be loaded and linked while an application is running. This has significant implications for resource management; multiple applications can use the same shared library without requiring duplicate copies in memory, leading to more efficient use of system resources. The linker determines which libraries to load, resolves any missing symbols, and ensures proper memory references.

Moreover, linkers can also incorporate linker scripts, which allow developers to customize the linking process. With linker scripts, developers can define how object files should be combined, specify the addresses for various segments in memory, and control the layout of the executable. This level of customization is particularly useful for embedded systems, where precise control over memory usage and layout can be a necessity due to resource constraints.

Linkers also interact closely with package managers in the Linux environment. Package managers automate the installation and configuration of libraries and other capabilities, creating dependencies that the linker needs to manage. When developers create software that relies on specific libraries, they must ensure that these libraries are correctly linked and accessible, reinforcing the need for effective dependency management during the linking phase.

The nature of linking in Linux further involves various strategies and techniques, particularly as practices have evolved over time with advancements in technology. Traditional static linking—which incorporates all necessary libraries and code into a single executable —provides speed and simplicity, whereas dynamic linking promotes flexibility by allowing resources to be shared and updated independently of the applications that use them. The right choice between these methods can impact performance significantly and must be made based on the needs and goals of the specific project.

Lastly, the evolution of linkers has mirrored the broader development of software practices. As programming languages and paradigms evolve, so too do linkers, adapting to support new methodologies, optimizations, and architectures in Linux development. During this evolution, the concepts of modular programming and object-oriented design have distinguished modern software development, underscoring the importance of linkers in facilitating this modular approach. By separating code into compartments and allowing independent development of components, linkers have become integral to achieving efficiency, reusability, and maintainability in software systems.

In conclusion, the linker is indispensable to the application development process on Linux systems. It seamlessly integrates code across multiple files and libraries, resolves references, and ensures that everything works together fluidly. By understanding how linkers function and their role in the development lifecycle, developers are better equipped to leverage the full capabilities of Linux libraries and to build high-performance, reliable applications that meet the diverse challenges of modern computing. Whether through optimizing linking strategies or judiciously managing dependencies, the exchanges between code and the linker manifest the hidden intricacies that drive the rich functionality found in Linux-based systems.

3. The History and Evolution of Linking in Linux

3.1. Early Days of Software Development

In the early days of software development, the landscape was markedly different from what modern developers experience today. The notion of linking—integrating and combining various pieces of code to create functional software—was still in its infancy. Before the advent of sophisticated operating systems like Linux, programming was often a rudimentary affair, dominated by low-level languages that required meticulous attention to detail, including memory management and assembly language.

The journey of software linking began in the era of mainframe computers and early programming languages such as assembly and Fortran. These languages lacked the abstraction layers that modern developers take for granted. Programmers worked directly with hardware addressing, creating programs that were tightly coupled to the specific architecture of each machine. This direct control, while offering high performance, also introduced considerable complexity and increased the potential for errors.

As software grew in complexity, the limitations of manually linking code became evident. Early compilation processes would generate object files, which were typically just collections of machine code without the sophisticated tools developers now rely on for assembly and linking. The need for a mechanism to correctly link multiple object files and resolve dependencies became apparent, leading to the development of linking methodologies.

From the late 1960s into the 1970s, as computer technology made strides, more advanced programming languages emerged, such as C. This period marked a significant turning point. The C language introduced the concept of modular programming, where code could be organized into separate files or modules. However, the assembly of these modules was not trivial. Each module contained its symbols— functions and variables—that needed resolving at compile time. This necessitated the design of a linking process that could effectively integrate different object files. Early linkers were relatively simple and performed straightforward tasks, such as merging object files into a single image.

The need for more complex linking became apparent with the advent of libraries, such as the C Standard Library, which encapsulated common routines that could be reused across programs. The idea of separating code into libraries and linking them at compile time or runtime urged the evolution of linking strategies. Meanwhile, programmers started to encounter challenges like symbol conflicts and variable scope rules when using external libraries. These complexities led to further innovations in linker design, including enhanced management of symbol visibility and resolution.

In the late 1970s and early 1980s, as operating systems evolved, the concept of dynamic linking began to take shape. Dynamic linking, a more flexible approach compared to its static counterpart, allowed for libraries to be loaded into memory only when needed. This capability not only reduced executable sizes but also enabled multiple programs to share a single library instance, yielding more efficient memory use and easier updates. However, early implementations posed challenges, especially regarding version control and ensuring consistent behavior across different application versions.

The transition to linking paradigms that embraced modularity and reuse set the stage for future developments, especially with the introduction of Unix and its successors, including Linux. As Unix established itself as a dominant operating system, linking practices began to mature. The design of Unix was inherently modular, and with it, the tradition of leveraging libraries grew stronger. Program components could be developed independently and linked together at runtime, promoting an ecosystem where shared resources could be managed effectively.

By the time Linux emerged in the early 1990s, more sophisticated models of linking had been established. Linkers evolved to support the more complex needs of multi-faceted software applications. The lessons learned from earlier linking practices became foundational. Linux embraced both static and dynamic linking strategies, optimizing for performance and flexibility. What had started as a straightforward procedure for combining object files had transformed into a critical component of software development, enabling the rich functionality that developers would leverage in their applications.

In summary, the early days of software development paved the way for the intricate linking methodologies that play a pivotal role in modern programming, especially in the Linux environment. From rudimentary assembly operations to the sophisticated linking techniques of today, the evolution of linking reflects both the progress in programming languages and the broader transformations in computing itself. Understanding this history equips developers with valuable insights into the principles that underpin current practices in linking, enabling them to appreciate the complexity and potential of the tools at their disposal in the Linux ecosystem.

3.2. The Birth of Linux

The story of Linux begins in 1991 with a Finnish computer science student named Linus Torvalds. As a student at the University of Helsinki, Torvalds sought to revolutionize his computing experience, inspired by the limitations he faced with the existing operating systems, particularly MINIX, which was designed primarily for educational purposes. Torvalds envisioned an operating system that was not only free but also open-source, which would allow developers worldwide to collaborate, innovate, and contribute to its growth.

From his initial experimentation, Torvalds began writing a kernel— what would become the heart of the Linux operating system. Unlike commercial operating systems that were often closed, proprietary, and restrictive, the Linux kernel was born out of a philosophy of sharing and collaboration. The early code was simple and sparse, focusing on the basic functionalities that would later expand into the vast and flexible Linux ecosystem. By releasing the kernel under the GNU General Public License (GPL), Torvalds invited developers to use, modify, and improve upon his work, reinforcing the belief that collaborative efforts could yield a robust and powerful operating system.

As the project gained traction, it quickly attracted a myriad of contributors who began porting essential libraries and developing applications to complement the growing kernel. Thus, with the inclusion of standard libraries—the GNU C Library (glibc) being particularly crucial—Linux began adopting new linking paradigms that facilitated not only the way code could be reused but also how it could interoperate across different programs seamlessly. The early decisions made regarding linking within Linux set the stage for the methodologies that would define the system in its later iterations.

One of the most significant innovations in linking that emerged from the Linux community was the concept of dynamic linking. This capability allowed the Linux operating system to load shared libraries at runtime rather than compile time. The advantages of dynamic libraries were manifold; they not only helped reduce the size of executables but also enabled multiple applications to share the same library code in memory. As a consequence, updates to libraries could be applied universally across all applications utilizing them without necessitating recompilation, which was not only a massive increase in efficiency but a key improvement in maintainability.

The introduction of dynamic linking in the Linux ecosystem represented a shift from traditional static linking approaches prevalent in early software development. While static linking—where libraries are included within the executable files—was straightforward, it came with its own set of challenges, such as bloating file sizes and complicating update procedures. By allowing applications to depend on shared resources instead of bundled copies, dynamic linking became a pivotal element in Linux's operational strategy.

The early releases of Linux garnered a supportive community fueled by the open-source ethos that encouraged experimentation. New libraries were developed to enhance functionality, and existing libraries were expanded, optimized, and integrated into the ecosystem. Developers began to establish best practices for linking, strategically organizing codebases into libraries that segmented functionalities, thus promoting modular design. The advanced linker capabilities evolved alongside this practice, with tools like the GNU linker (ld) providing mechanisms to streamline the linking process.

Furthermore, the burgeoning Linux operating system benefitted enormously from collaborative platforms like the Free Software Foundation, which provided the philosophical underpinning for addressing software licensing and promoting the idea of free software. The dynamic interplay between the kernel's growth and the development of libraries ushered in an innovative environment characterized by rapid technological advancements.

As Linux matured through the 1990s and early 2000s, the role of linking continued to evolve. The rise of more complex applications, often interconnected and reliant on multiple libraries, necessitated sophisticated linking techniques capable of addressing performance, compatibility, and dependency issues. Developers increasingly emphasized the importance of efficient linking practices that could optimize resource utilization in a world increasingly reliant on software solutions spanning a multitude of devices and uses.

Not only did linking become vital in ensuring that libraries were effectively utilized, but it also prompted innovations such as linker scripts that allowed developers to customize how libraries were linked at a very granular level. This capability became critical, especially in environments like embedded systems or real-time applications, where resource management and performance requirements could not just be an afterthought.

The evolution of caching mechanisms, lazy loading techniques, and improved debugging tools such as Valgrind and GDB bolstered developers' capabilities to optimize and troubleshoot linked applications seamlessly. Through this carefully woven tapestry of collaboration, innovation, and optimization, Linux transformed into a powerful and versatile operating system, underpinned by a rich ecosystem of linked libraries and applications.

Thus, the birth of Linux was not just the inception of a new operating system; it marked the introduction of new paradigms in linking methods and methodologies that would profoundly influence how software was developed, shared, and executed. This foundational shift continues to shape the landscape of software development today, illustrating the longstanding impact of Linux on the world of programming and its commitment to open collaboration and innovation.

3.3. Transformation through Innovation

In examining the transformation of Linux linking and its myriad developments over the decades, it is abundant that innovations have not only revolutionized linking methodologies but also influenced the broader landscape of software development within the Linux ecosystem. The evolution of linking can be traced through several key milestones that highlight remarkable advances and pivotal shifts in how linking has been approached, understood, and leveraged.

The transition from static to dynamic linking marked one of the most significant milestones in the history of Linux linking. Static linking, wherein all required libraries are included within the executable at compile time, was once the standard approach, offering simplicity and performance advantages in certain applications. However, as software grew increasingly complex—with vast dependencies and a need for frequent updates—the limitations of static linking became starkly evident. Executable files became bloated, necessitating recompilation with every library update, which was both time-consuming and error-prone. This prompted a rethinking of linking strategies, leading to the adoption of dynamic linking.

Dynamic linking enabled a paradigm shift by allowing libraries to be loaded into memory at runtime. Multiple applications could utilize a single instance of a shared library without duplicating code, leading to significant memory savings and easier application updates. This welcomed a new era characterized by flexibility and modularity, empowering developers to create applications that could evolve rapidly without the overhead associated with statically linked dependencies. The implications of dynamic linking were far-reaching, emphasizing not just efficiency but also the ease of collaborative development, as shared libraries promoted the reuse of code across different applications, driving innovation.

To further streamline the development process, innovations in linker technologies emerged, such as link-time optimization (LTO) techniques. These techniques enhance performance by allowing the compiler to perform optimizations at the linking stage, rather than solely at the compilation stage. By considering the entire program in its entirety, link-time optimization can lead to more efficient binary code, reducing runtime overhead and improving overall application performance. Such advancements underscore a transformative shift towards more aggressive optimizations that capitalize on the power of modern computing architectures.

The advent of comprehensive package management systems within Linux distributions has also vastly contributed to the landscape of linking. Package managers facilitate the installation, upgrade, and management of software and libraries, introducing a level of automation and consistency that was previously unattainable. This systematization helps mitigate the dependency issue that often arises with libraries, ensuring that compatible versions are used and conflicts are resolved efficiently. The integration of package managers with the linker further enhances the developer experience, creating an ecosystem where libraries can be easily shared and maintained.

Another notable transformation is found in the realm of cross-compilation and linking. As the demand for software to run across a plethora of devices—from embedded systems to cloud services—has surged, cross-compilation techniques have evolved. Developers can now build software for different architectures, ensuring that applications can be deployed across diverse systems while appropriately managing linking requirements. This sophistication in cross-compilation has opened doors for portability and flexibility that have become essential in today's multi-platform environments.

The emergence of advanced debugging and profiling tools has profoundly influenced how linking issues are identified and resolved within Linux. Programs such as GDB and Valgrind allow developers to diagnose linking errors effectively, track memory usage, and optimize performance. These tools have become invaluable for maintaining the integrity of linked applications, supporting developers in cleaning up dependencies and ensuring optimal operation without wasting resources.

Additionally, security considerations have necessitated innovations in linking processes. As the threat landscapes evolve, linkers have integrated security features that ensure vulnerabilities in shared libraries are systematically addressed and mitigated. Techniques such as position-independent code (PIC) and address space layout randomization (ASLR) have made linked applications more resilient against attacks, securing memory allocation dynamically and thereby increasing the overall safety of executing linked programs.

The influence of community-driven open source contributions cannot be overlooked when discussing transformation through innovation in Linux linking. The collaborative ethos amongst Linux developers has resulted in rapid sharing of best practices, enhancement of existing libraries, and pioneering of new approaches to linking. This network of collaboration has fostered an environment where knowledge is freely exchanged, and innovation flourishes, propelling the Linux ecosystem into a dynamic frontier of possibilities.

As we stand on the cusp of further technological transformations, the foundations laid through these innovations continue to propel the Linux ecosystem forward. Future developments in artificial intelligence and machine learning may lead to intelligent linking mechanisms, where the linking process is automated and optimized based on usage patterns and application demands. The embrace of containerization technologies, including Docker and Kubernetes, may also prompt new linking paradigms tailored specifically to microservices architecture.

Ultimately, the journey of linking within Linux reflects a larger narrative of adaptation and growth. The innovations witnessed over the years—ranging from dynamic linking techniques to advanced tooling, intelligent optimizations, and community collaboration—have not only enhanced the capabilities of Linux libraries but have also ensured that they remain at the forefront of modern software development. This dynamic interplay of innovation will continue to shape the trajectory of linking in Linux, empowering developers to harness libraries and linking practices to create efficient, resilient, and highly functional applications in a landscape that is perpetually evolving.

3.4. Modern Linking Techniques

In the evolving landscape of software development, modern linking techniques have emerged as a key area of focus for developers and system architects working within Linux environments. These techniques are designed to optimize the linking process, enhancing performance, flexibility, and usability. As applications have grown in complexity, the methods and tools available for linking have had to adapt, integrating advanced strategies that cater to contemporary development needs.

At the core of modern linking is the balance between static and dynamic linking. Static linking involves combining all library files into a single executable at compile time, resulting in an all-in-one binary. While static linking offers certain performance benefits—such as quicker load times and independence from library availability —it also presents significant challenges. For example, maintaining updated versions of libraries requires recompiling dependent applications, which can be tedious and error-prone.

Conversely, dynamic linking allows programs to share libraries at runtime. This flexibility leads to reduced executable sizes and memory usage, as the same library can be utilized by multiple applications simultaneously. Furthermore, when a shared library is updated, all applications relying on it can take advantage of improvements without needing recompilation. This strategy emphasizes efficiency and promotes maintainability, crucial in high-availability systems where uptime is paramount.

Over the years, the techniques for managing these linking strategies have become increasingly sophisticated. Modern linkers often incorporate optimizations during the linking process—such as link-time optimization (LTO)—which analyze the entire codebase at link time. By doing this, linkers can apply optimizations across modules, allowing for more efficient code execution and enhanced application performance. This increase in efficiency is particularly valuable in performance-centric environments, where even the smallest overhead can significantly impact responsiveness.

The evolution of package management systems has greatly impacted modern linking strategies. Tools like APT, YUM, and Pacman provide developers and system administrators with comprehensive methods to install, update, and manage software libraries while automatically handling dependencies. These package managers not only simplify library management but also ensure that libraries are compatible with the applications using them, mitigating the complications often associated with library conflicts.

Furthermore, the introduction of linker scripts allows developers to exercise a greater degree of control over the linking process. With linker scripts, developers can dictate the order of linking, specify memory addresses, and control the layout of the final executable. This level of customization can be vital in embedded systems or real-time applications, where memory management is crucial and every byte counts. By preparing targeting-specific linker scripts, developers can optimize performance and tailor applications to meet specific operational requirements.

Real-time systems, in particular, benefit from modern linking techniques that prioritize swift execution and predictability. Techniques that minimize linking overhead—which is critical in scenarios demanding consistent response times—are essential for ensuring that real-time applications function as intended. This is reflected in the development of linking methods designed specifically for environments where latency is a primary concern, balancing the need for flexibility and speed.

Security in linking is another focal point for modern techniques. As linking often involves using third-party libraries, ensuring that these libraries are secure is critical to safeguarding applications from vulnerabilities. Developers are encouraged to adopt best practices such as verifying library sources, maintaining regular updates, and potentially employing security frameworks that scan for weaknesses within linked libraries before deployment. Modern linkers have begun incorporating security features that facilitate the detection of issues and enhance overall robustness.

In addition, cross-compilation techniques have evolved to accommodate the prolific use of embedded devices and Internet of Things (IoT) systems, where software must run on diverse hardware architectures. Modern linking practices ensure that applications can seamlessly transition across platforms, judiciously managing libraries pertinent to the specific environment. By handling dependencies with cross-architecture considerations, modern linking techniques enable broader application reach and versatility.

Finally, engaging with open-source communities fosters collaboration that fuels innovation in modern linking techniques. Developers share advancements, suggest optimizations, and contribute to benchmarking efforts, leading to a collective enhancement of linking practices. Such collaborative environments yield a continual refinement of techniques and tools that address contemporary challenges faced by developers working in complex ecosystems.

In conclusion, modern linking techniques in Linux have undergone a transformation driven by the need for efficiency, flexibility, security, and ease of maintenance in software development. As the demands on software applications evolve, so too do the strategies and tools available to developers. Through a combination of static and dynamic linking, advanced linker optimizations, robust package management systems, customizable linker scripts, attentive security practices, and cross-compilation capabilities, the landscape of linking in Linux continues to adapt, ensuring that it remains relevant and effective in powering the next generation of applications. Understanding and leveraging these modern techniques is crucial for developers aiming to build high-performance, maintainable software that meets the dynamic needs of today's computing environment.

4. Static Libraries: Foundations and Applications

4.1. Creating Static Libraries

Creating static libraries is a crucial skill for developers working within the Linux ecosystem. A static library is a collection of object files that are linked into an application at compile time, effectively becoming a part of the executable itself. Unlike dynamic libraries, which are loaded at runtime, static libraries provide the advantage of self-contained binaries that do not require additional dependencies at execution. This process of creating static libraries involves a series of well-defined steps, conditions, and practices that enhance the efficiency and maintainability of applications.

To create a static library in Linux, you first need to compile your source code files (.c or .cpp) into object files (.o). This can be achieved using the GNU Compiler Collection (GCC). The syntax for compiling a source file into an object file is as follows:

```
gcc -c source_file.c -o source_file.o
```

The -c option tells the compiler to generate an object file rather than an executable. This process can be repeated for each source file in your project. For instance, if you have multiple source files like file1.c, file2.c, and file3.c, you would compile each one into its corresponding object file.

Once you have your object files created, you can use the ar command to bundle them into a static library. The ar command is a Unix utility that creates, modifies, and extracts from archives, which in this context means assembling the object files into a library archive file. The general syntax for creating a static library is:

```
ar rcs libmylibrary.a file1.o file2.o file3.o
```

The r flag tells ar to insert the files into the archive, the c flag creates the archive if it does not already exist, and the s flag generates an index for quick access to the library's contents. The resulting library is saved as `libmylibrary.a`, where the "lib" prefix is a convention in C and C++ programming that indicates it's a library file.

After creating the static library, you may want to check its contents to ensure that it was created successfully. The command to list the files in the library is:

```
ar t libmylibrary.a
```

This will display the object files that are included in the library. Additionally, you can use the `nm` command to view the symbols defined in the library. This can be particularly useful for debugging purposes:

```
nm libmylibrary.a
```

Once you have your static library created and verified, you can link it to your application. This step involves specifying the static library when compiling your program using GCC. The syntax for linking a static library is similar to linking other object files, with the following command:

```
gcc main.c -L. -lmylibrary -o myapplication
```

In this command, `-L.` tells the linker to look for the library in the current directory, and `-lmylibrary` specifies the name of the library. Note that the prefix `lib` is omitted, and the suffix `.a` is also not included.

It's important to understand that static linking contributes to the overall size of your final executable, as all the necessary object code from the library is incorporated into it. Therefore, while static libraries bring the independence of runtime linking and can enhance performance for certain applications, this inclusion can lead to larger binary sizes and may complicate the update process if changes to the library are necessary. Any change in the library will indeed require recompiling the application to reflect those updates.

In summary, creating static libraries involves compiling source files into object files, using the `ar` utility to bundle them into a library archive, verifying the library's contents, and finally linking that library into your application. This straightforward yet powerful process is fundamental to many projects within the Linux development environment, enabling modularity, code reuse, and structured application design. Mastering the creation of static libraries empowers developers to build robust software while maintaining efficiency and performance throughout the development lifecycle.

4.2. Linking with Static Libraries

Linking with static libraries is an essential process that developers engage in while building applications in the Linux environment. This process allows developers to incorporate precompiled code into their executables, making applications self-contained and reducing reliance on external dependencies at runtime. The procedure involves several stages, including the creation, usage, and configuration of static libraries, which are critical for ensuring applications function correctly and efficiently.

To effectively link with static libraries, one must first understand how to create them. Static libraries are essentially collections of object files, which contain machine code derived from source code files. The typical steps for creating a static library begin with compiling the source code. Using the GNU Compiler Collection (GCC), you can generate object files from your source files, using a command such as:

gcc -c mysourcefile.c -o mysourcefile.o

Here, the -c flag instructs GCC to compile the source file into an object file without linking. Once you have compiled all necessary source files into object files, the next step is to create a static library using the ar command. This command is used as follows:

ar rcs libmylibrary.a myobjectfile1.o myobjectfile2.o

In this example, the -rcs flags signify that you are creating a new library (r) and updating its index (s). The resulting output is a static library named libmylibrary.a. Once the library is created, it can be verified using commands like ar t libmylibrary.a, which lists the contents, or nm `libmylibrary.a`, which displays the symbols defined within the library.

After creating the static library, the next critical step is to link it to your application. This process is usually carried out during the compilation of the main executable. You can link the static library to your application with the following command:

gcc main_application.c -L. -lmylibrary -o myapplication

In this command, `-L.` specifies the current directory as the location of the library, while `-lmylibrary` indicates the linker to look for the `libmylibrary.a` static library. Note that the `lib` prefix and the `.a` suffix are omitted in the linking command.

One key advantage of using static libraries is that they create a self-contained executable. Once the application is compiled and linked with the static library, there is no further need for the library at run-time. This can lead to performance benefits, particularly in scenarios requiring fast, predictable execution, as all functions are resolved during the compile time. Furthermore, statically linked applications can avoid the common pitfalls associated with dynamic libraries, such as library version conflicts and missing dependencies.

However, leveraging static libraries does come with trade-offs. The most significant downside is the increased size of the final executable since all the code from the linked libraries is included in the binary. As a result, deploying multiple versions of an application using the same library can lead to redundancy, consuming more disk space and memory resources. Additionally, if the static library undergoes an update—be it bug fixes, performance improvements, or new features —every application that depends on it must be recompiled to take advantage of these changes, which can be a cumbersome process in larger systems.

Despite these challenges, static libraries are invaluable in specific scenarios where predictability, performance, and independence are paramount. For instance, in embedded systems or environments where memory constraints are present, developers often prefer static libraries due to their self-contained nature and reduced runtime overhead.

Managing static libraries within a project involves keeping track of the versions used, ensuring compatibility, and organizing source files and object files systematically. Proper documentation and adherence to naming conventions can significantly ease the burden of library management.

In summary, linking with static libraries is a foundational practice in Linux programming that serves to enhance the self-sufficiency, efficiency, and performance of applications. Understanding how to create and manage static libraries empowers developers to build robust software while balancing the trade-offs associated with static linking, leading to high-quality applications that meet the performance demands of today's computing environments.

4.3. Benefits of Static Libraries

Static libraries play a pivotal role in performance enhancement within software applications, particularly in the context of Linux environments. When developers choose to employ static libraries, they significantly impact the overall efficiency, speed, and reliability of their applications. The core advantage of using static libraries lies in their operational characteristics, which provide self-contained binaries that integrate all necessary components into a single executable at compile time. This characteristic confers several benefits worth exploring in detail.

To begin with, the performance of applications linked with static libraries is generally enhanced due to the avoidance of dynamic resolution. When an application is compiled with static libraries, all required object code is bundled into the executable at build time. This leads to immediate symbol resolution, where all function calls are resolved during the compilation process, thereby reducing the overhead that might occur during execution. Unlike dynamic libraries, which require loading and linking at runtime, static libraries ensure that all necessary resources are readily available within the executable, resulting in faster startup times and improved execution speed. In environments where performance is paramount, such as high-frequency trading algorithms or real-time monitoring applications, this characteristic provides a distinct edge.

Another significant advantage is the elimination of runtime dependencies. Statically linked applications can operate independently of the underlying system libraries once compiled. This independence is particularly beneficial when deploying applications across varied environments where library versions may differ or where certain libraries may not be installed at all. The statically linked executable embodies everything it requires, ensuring reliability without the potential for "dependency hell," a term that describes the challenges arising from managing numerous interdependent library versions. This resolution of dependencies at compile time ensures that the application is portable, making deployment straightforward in diverse environments, from testing to production.

Moreover, static libraries contribute to security advantages by encapsulating all required code within the application. This encapsulation limits the number of external dependencies, inherently reducing the surface area for potential vulnerabilities that could be exploited through dynamic linking. When applications rely on shared dynamic libraries, they may inadvertently expose themselves to risks if those libraries contain security flaws—flaws that could be targeted if the library was compromised. By using static libraries, developers mitigate these risks, ensuring a more controlled and secure execution environment.

Additionally, the use of static libraries can lead to a more efficient memory footprint, especially in cases where the same static library is utilized across multiple applications. While each application will contain its copy of the library in its final executable, this approach can be beneficial in tightly controlled systems where ensuring consistency is more critical than minimizing disk space. In scenarios where the same applications or libraries are frequently executed, caching mechanisms employed by the operating system can optimize memory usage further, making the performance gains more pronounced.

Beyond mere performance gains, static libraries facilitate better debugging experiences. Since all code required for execution is compiled into a single binary, it simplifies the debugging process. Developers can analyze the entire application with tools such as gdb without needing to consider multiple library versions. This aspect can significantly streamline the troubleshooting process, making it easier to reproduce errors and trace issues within the application. The compounded visibility of the code increases maintainability and reduces the chances of version-related errors going undetected.

Furthermore, adopting static libraries fosters a culture of reliability and version control among teams. Statically linking libraries provides a clear understanding of what version of a library is being used in an application, eliminating ambiguity that can arise from dynamically linked libraries. This clarity can enhance team collaboration, as developers can document and track the specific versions of libraries embedded in their executables, promoting a more systematic approach to software maintenance and updates.

Despite the numerous advantages outlined, static libraries do come with trade-offs that developers need to consider. One of the most notable is the increase in binary size, as all used code from the static libraries is integrated into the final executable. This integral nature can complicate distribution in terms of both storage requirements and bandwidth consumption during deployment, which may become problematic for applications intended for resource-constrained environments or in scenarios requiring rapid deployment over slow networks.

On the other hand, managing updates becomes cumbersome with static libraries. Should a bug be discovered in a static library, each dependent application must be recompiled with the newer version to benefit from the fix. This limitation can lengthen development cycles and may hinder responsiveness to security vulnerabilities, particularly in large projects with many dependencies.

In conclusion, the benefits of static libraries extend beyond mere performance improvements; they encompass a wide range of attributes that collectively enhance the reliability, maintainability, and security of Linux applications. As the software development landscape continues to evolve, the importance of understanding and strategically utilizing static libraries remains a fundamental aspect for developers. Balancing the inherent trade-offs associated with static linking while maximizing its advantages is essential for achieving optimal performance in modern applications. This nuanced approach to linking within the Linux ecosystem enables developers to harness the full power and capabilities of static libraries, ultimately leading to robust and high-performing software solutions.

4.4. Challenges and Limitations

In the pursuit of utilizing static libraries within application development, several challenges and limitations must be acknowledged, despite the numerous benefits they offer. Such constraints can significantly influence a developer's decision-making process when architecting applications, especially within the complex landscape of the Linux ecosystem.

One of the primary limitations of static libraries is the increased size of the executable files generated from them. When a programmer links a static library to an application, all the necessary object files from that library are incorporated directly into the final binary. This results in larger executable sizes compared to dynamically linked applications, which only contain references to shared libraries. In scenarios where memory and storage are premium, such as in embedded systems or devices with limited resources, this increase can prove problematic. Larger executables require more disk space and can also lead to longer load times when all the functions and code are being loaded into memory at runtime, which could deter users accustomed to faster, more streamlined applications.

Moreover, the inherent nature of static libraries necessitates that any updates or changes made to the library itself require recompilation of all dependent applications. If a bug is fixed or a new feature is introduced in the static library, developers must rebuild and redeploy every application that uses it to ensure that those changes are reflected. This process can become cumbersome and time-consuming, particularly in large-scale applications or when multiple developers are working on various components. The potential for inconsistency between library versions can result in errors, and managing these varying versions can degrade the maintenance experience, leading to a condition known as "dependency hell." This occurs when applications unknowingly depend on different versions of the same library, resulting in various compatibility issues that are challenging to address.

In addition to the challenges of version management, static linking brings forward the risk of code bloat. Since all required code is bundled into the main executable, the same library applied across multiple applications leads to redundancy. Each time a developer creates a new static link with the same library, it incorporates a duplicate of the library's content, consuming additional disk space and potentially leading to inefficient memory usage. This is particularly evident in environments where many applications share similar library functions. In contrast, dynamic libraries allow for shared access across applications, yielding more economical resource utilization.

Static libraries also pose a challenge in ensuring that applications remain portable. Applications statically linked to libraries can work seamlessly in controlled environments where the library has not changed. However, in production scenarios, where the hardware and operating systems may vary, the uniformity of static libraries may produce unexpected dependencies on specific compiler versions and settings. As libraries evolve, developers must ensure they are keeping up with their static library implementations, leading to increased maintenance overhead.

Another limitation lies in the debugging process. While static libraries can simplify debugging since all required code is integrated into a single executable, they can also obscure the debugging of issues stemming from library codes. Statically linking a problematic library means that developers may face difficulty tracing an error back to the specific lines in the library code, particularly in scenarios where the library is expansive. This complexity introduces challenges for maintainers who need to comprehend the interplay between library code and application logic for efficient troubleshooting.

Security considerations also surface as a significant aspect of static library usage. Although static linking can mitigate risks associated with dynamic library exploits—such as vulnerabilities within shared libraries—it does not eliminate them altogether. When an application is built using a static library, vulnerabilities present in the library code are packaged into the application. Moreover, updating these libraries to address vulnerabilities necessitates recompiling the entire application once again. This delay can expose applications to security risks for extended periods, especially if they are deployed in environments with stringent uptime requirements and limited maintenance windows.

Lastly, the licensing of static libraries can present complexities. Many static libraries, particularly those from open-source projects, come with specific licensing agreements that dictate how they may be used or modified. Developers must navigate these licenses carefully to ensure compliance, as failing to do so can lead to legal challenges or violations that may jeopardize a project or organization. This becomes particularly intricate when multiple libraries, each under differing licenses, are used in conjunction, requiring thorough understanding and awareness of the implications involved.

In summary, while static libraries provide significant advantages in terms of performance, independence, and reliability, they also introduce a range of challenges and limitations. These include increased executable sizes, cumbersome update processes, code bloat, portability issues, debugging difficulties, potential security vulnerabilities, and complex licensing considerations. A nuanced understanding of these factors is crucial for developers when making decisions regarding library utilization in the context of the broader architecture of their applications within the Linux ecosystem. Balancing the inherent benefits with the associated challenges allows for the prudent design, efficient maintenance, and secure operation of software solutions that leverage static libraries effectively.

5. Dynamic Libraries: Flexibility and Power

5.1. Dynamic versus Static Linking

Dynamic and static linking are two fundamental mechanisms that influence how software applications utilize libraries in Linux environments. Understanding the distinction between the two can greatly impact the design and performance of software solutions, as each approach possesses its unique advantages and drawbacks.

Static linking involves the inclusion of all necessary library code into a single executable file during the compile time. When a developer compiles code that uses a static library, a copy of the library's code is directly incorporated into the final binary. The resulting executable is thus self-contained and does not depend on external libraries at runtime. This characteristic provides certain benefits, such as simplified deployment since all required code is bundled together. Furthermore, static libraries tend to result in faster execution speeds because all symbol resolutions occur at compile time, eliminating the overhead associated with dynamically loaded libraries during application startup.

However, static linking also has limitations. One of the most significant drawbacks is the increased size of the executable. As each application that links against a static library includes its own copy of the library's code, storage requirements can escalate, which is a concern in resource-constrained environments. Additionally, any updates to the library necessitate recompiling and redeploying all applications that rely on it. This can lead to issues with maintaining consistency and manageability when numerous applications depend on the same library, especially in large-scale systems.

Dynamic linking, on the other hand, allows for the separation of library code from the application itself. Shared libraries are loaded into memory during runtime, allowing multiple applications to utilize the same library instance concurrently. This approach fosters memory efficiency, as the operating system only loads one copy of the library code into memory, significantly reducing overall utilization. Dynamic linking also facilitates easier updates; when a library is updated, all applications that depend on it automatically benefit from the changes, provided they are compatible with the new version. This flexibility enhances maintainability and reduces deployment overhead, which is particularly advantageous in environments that experience frequent updates.

Despite these benefits, dynamic linking introduces complexities in terms of dependency management. When an application starts, the dynamic linker must resolve all library dependencies, which can lead to issues if the required versions of libraries are not present or if there are conflicts between different library versions. This phenomenon often referred to as "dependency hell," poses challenges in ensuring that applications operate seamlessly across various environments. Moreover, the reliance on shared libraries means that applications may encounter undefined behavior if a critical library is missing or if an incompatible version is inadvertently installed.

The choice between static and dynamic linking typically hinges on the specific requirements of a project and its deployment environment. For performance-critical applications where execution speed and memory usage are paramount, static linking may be preferred despite the increase in binary size. Conversely, for projects that require frequent updates, dynamic linking offers a more agile solution, promoting rapid deployment cycles without the need for recompilation.

In summary, dynamic and static linking mechanisms each present unique characteristics and operational implications within the Linux ecosystem. Static linking provides self-contained executables that enhance performance but complicate updates, while dynamic linking fosters flexibility and resource management at the cost of potential dependency challenges. A nuanced understanding of these mechanisms is essential for developers as they decide how to structure their software applications, ensuring that they select the optimal linking strategy that aligns with their project goals and deployment scenarios.

5.2. Benefits of Dynamic Libraries

Dynamic libraries have revolutionized the efficiency and flexibility of software development, particularly in the context of Linux environments. The benefits of utilizing dynamic libraries extend beyond mere code reuse; they offer significant advantages that can enhance both performance and maintenance across various applications. A dynamic library, or shared library, is a collection of code that is loaded into memory at runtime, allowing multiple programs to access shared functions and routines without the need for each program to contain its own copy. This unique characteristic lays the foundation for several compelling benefits.

One of the most significant advantages of dynamic libraries is memory efficiency. In traditional static linking, every executable file contains its own copy of the library code it depends upon, leading to the accumulation of redundancy across applications. This not only inflates the size of individual binaries but also results in inefficient memory usage, as the same library code is unnecessarily loaded multiple times into RAM. Dynamic libraries address this issue by allowing multiple applications to share a single instance of the library in memory. Consequently, the operating system can load the library code only once, which drastically reduces the overall memory footprint of running applications. This is particularly advantageous in environments where numerous applications are simultaneously active, leading to improved resource management and system performance.

In addition to improving memory utilization, dynamic libraries enhance software modularity and maintainability. When developers make updates or bug fixes to a dynamic library, all applications utilizing that library can benefit from the enhancements immediately, without requiring recompilation of every dependent program. This results in a more streamlined update process and ensures that applications can be kept current with the latest features and security patches. For system administrators and developers alike, this independence from recompilation facilitates rapid deployment cycles and simplifies version management. In large-scale applications, where maintaining consistency across several deployments is critical, this feature can significantly reduce operational overhead.

The advantages of dynamic libraries extend beyond mere memory and maintenance; they enhance the user experience as well. Applications linked with dynamic libraries can boast faster startup times since not all library code needs to be loaded into memory at once; instead, it is loaded progressively as needed during execution. This delay in loading non-critical library functions can result in a more responsive application, particularly beneficial in user interface-heavy applications where user experience is paramount.

Dynamic libraries also encourage a culture of collaboration and innovation within the development community. Many key libraries in the Linux ecosystem are open-source, allowing developers to contribute to and enhance them over time. This communal approach not only enriches the libraries but also encourages a shared understanding of coding practices and methodologies. By relying on widely-used dynamic libraries, developers can leverage collective knowledge and experience, enabling them to develop applications that are more secure and feature-rich.

Moreover, dynamic linking enables developers to implement advanced techniques such as plugin architectures and runtime polymorphism. By designing applications that leverage dynamic libraries, developers can create extensible systems where new functionality can be added without altering the core codebase. This flexibility is crucial in environments that demand adaptability and rapid response to changing user needs.

Another noteworthy benefit of dynamic libraries is the facilitation of internationalization and localization. When a core application is developed with dynamic libraries, adding support for different languages or cultural nuances can often be as simple as swapping out specific libraries for others designed for localization. This modularity simplifies the task of making applications accessible to a global audience, a necessity in today's interconnected world.

Despite the numerous strengths of dynamic libraries, they are not without challenges. Dependency management becomes critical, as applications relying on specific versions of libraries may face conflicts if those libraries are updated. The infamous "dependency hell" can arise if two applications require different versions of the same shared library, necessitating careful management and consideration for compatibility. Additionally, developers should be vigilant about ensuring that the necessary shared libraries are available on target systems, particularly when deploying applications on different Linux distributions or configurations.

Security is another area that requires attention. Dynamic libraries, while offering sharing benefits, can expose applications to vulnerabilities specific to the libraries they depend upon. If a shared library is compromised, all applications relying on it may also become susceptible to attacks. This necessitates the importance of maintaining updated and secure libraries, as well as employing best practices for software development that minimize the chances of exploitation.

In conclusion, the benefits of dynamic libraries in the Linux environment are multifaceted and substantial. They provide significant advantages in memory efficiency, modularity, maintainability, and user experience while fostering collaboration within the development community. Dynamic libraries' flexibility supports advanced programming techniques and simplifies internationalization, making them a vital component of modern software development. However, developers must remain vigilant about managing dependencies, ensuring security, and actively keeping libraries updated to fully harness the advantages dynamic libraries offer. As the landscape of software development continues to evolve, leveraging dynamic libraries will remain a cornerstone for building robust, efficient applications that meet the diverse needs of users and organizations alike.

5.3. Creating and Managing Dynamic Libraries

Creating and managing dynamic libraries is an essential component of software development in Linux. Dynamic libraries, also known as shared libraries, allow developers to write modular code that is both efficient and easy to maintain. Unlike static libraries, which are linked and compiled into the final executable at build time, dynamic libraries are loaded at runtime, enabling several advantages such as smaller executable sizes and ease of updating shared code.

To create a dynamic library in Linux, developers typically follow a structured process. The first step involves writing the source code files that contain the functions and methods intended for inclusion in the library. These files are usually written in languages like C or C++. After the source code is developed, the next step is to compile these files into position-independent code (PIC). PIC is crucial for shared libraries because it allows the library functions to be loaded at any memory address, which is essential for efficient memory management.

To compile source files into PIC, developers use the gcc (GNU Compiler Collection) with the -fPIC option. For instance, if you have a source file named mylibrary.c, you would run the following command:

```
gcc -fPIC -c mylibrary.c -o mylibrary.o
```

This command compiles the mylibrary.c file into an object file named mylibrary.o, ensuring that the resulting object code is position-independent.

Following this step, developers will package the object files into a shared library using the gcc tool again, this time with the -shared option. The command to create a shared library is as follows:

```
gcc -shared -o libmylibrary.so mylibrary.o
```

This command generates a shared library called libmylibrary.so, where "lib" is the conventional prefix for library files and ".so" indicates that it is a shared object. The shared library can now be used by multiple applications, which can dynamically link to it when they are run.

Once a shared library is created, it is crucial to manage its dependencies effectively. Developers must ensure that any application using this library is aware of its location and can find it at runtime. When an application is run, the dynamic linker (often `ld.so` on Linux) searches for shared libraries that the application depends on in specified locations. Typically, developers place shared libraries in standard directories such as `/usr/lib`, but custom paths can be set using the `LD_LIBRARY_PATH` environment variable or by configuring the dynamic linker's run-time bindings through the `ld.so.conf` file.

Managing dynamic libraries requires an understanding of versioning and compatibility. As libraries evolve with bug fixes or enhancements, maintaining backward compatibility is vital to avoid breaking existing applications. Developers can use versioning techniques, including version script files that define symbols to be exported from shared libraries, to ensure that applications using older versions continue to function correctly. By defining versioning attributes during the library creation process, developers can track changes and maintain multiple versions of the same library on the system.

Another aspect of managing dynamic libraries involves using various tools to diagnose and troubleshoot library-related issues. Linux offers a variety of command-line tools, such as `ldd`, which displays the shared library dependencies of an executable. This can help developers understand which libraries are required for running their applications. The command `ldd ./myapplication` will show all the shared libraries dynamically linked with the `myapplication` executable.

Furthermore, memory and performance profiling tools, such as `valgrind`, can be used for assessing the efficiency of dynamic libraries. They can help identify memory leaks or wasted memory from object allocation, ensuring that the dynamic libraries are optimized for performance.

One of the biggest advantages of using dynamic libraries is the ability to update shared code without recompiling dependent applications. With dynamic linking, if a library is updated with new features or bug fixes, all applications using that library can benefit from the update immediately upon restart. This feature greatly simplifies the maintenance process in production environments where ease of updates is crucial to minimize downtime.

However, managing dynamic libraries also presents certain challenges. Dependency management is crucial, as applications may fall into "dependency hell" when they require different versions of the same library. This situation can be mitigated through proper versioning strategies, utilizing package managers, or employing containerization technologies to isolate application environments.

In conclusion, creating and managing dynamic libraries is a sophisticated yet vital practice for developers in the Linux ecosystem. By understanding how to structure code for dynamic linking, compile shared libraries appropriately, and manage dependencies, developers can enhance both the efficiency and maintainability of their applications. With the right tools and practices in place, dynamic libraries not only contribute to a cleaner and more modular codebase but also support a more agile development process that can adapt to changing requirements and priorities over time.

5.4. Loading Shared Libraries at Runtime

Loading shared libraries at runtime is a fundamental aspect of dynamic linking that allows applications to engage with predefined libraries without having to include all the necessary code within the binary itself. This feature is particularly critical in Linux environments, where the flexibility and efficiency of shared libraries have become essential for modern software development.

When an application is executed, it does not include all of its library code directly within its executable file. Instead, it relies on the dynamic linker to load the necessary shared libraries into memory at runtime. This process begins with the execution of the application binary, which contains metadata about the libraries it requires. This metadata is provided in the form of an ELF (Executable and Linkable Format) header that is also a part of the Linux binary format. The ELF header includes details like the entry point of the program, the section headers, and section names, as well as a list of shared libraries the binary depends on.

The dynamic linker, most commonly `ld-linux.so`, is the system component responsible for locating and loading these shared libraries. Upon the launch of an executable, the operating system invokes the dynamic linker, which examines the binary's header and determines which shared libraries need to be loaded into memory. It then resolves the locations of these libraries based on several criteria, such as default library paths, the system's configured library directories, and any environment variables that might influence the library loading process, like `LD_LIBRARY_PATH`.

As the dynamic linker starts loading the necessary libraries, it performs a series of checks and verifications. For example, it verifies that each library is compatible with the application, checking for versioning prerequisites and available symbols that the application expects to use. This verification process helps prevent runtime errors due to missing symbols or incompatible versions, effectively allowing the system to maintain stability even when libraries are updated or changed.

Another vital step in loading shared libraries is the process of symbol resolution. Each object file and shared library contains symbols, which are references to functions or variables. During runtime, the dynamic linker needs to bind these symbols correctly, ensuring that function calls in the application point to the correct locations in the loaded libraries. This process involves matching the unresolved symbols in the executable with the resolutions available in the loaded shared libraries. If all symbols are successfully resolved, the dynamic linker creates a symbol table that allows the application to reference these symbols as needed during execution.

The efficiency of shared libraries is notably enhanced by the concept of copy-on-write memory management used in modern operating systems. When shared libraries are loaded into memory, the kernel maps them to the memory pages of the executing processes. This means that the code from shared libraries is not duplicated for each process that uses it; rather, all processes share the same code in memory, significantly saving on memory resources. Each process has its own copy of the data segments that may change during execution, but the executable code remains shared. This is particularly beneficial in environments where many applications run simultaneously, as it reduces the overall memory footprint.

Moreover, the dynamic linker also implements additional features to optimize performance and resource management. For instance, lazy loading allows the dynamic linker to only load the shared library when a function defined in that library is actually called. This optimized approach can lead to faster application startup times because the overhead associated with loading libraries is only incurred if and when needed. This technique is particularly useful in applications with extensive dependencies, where not all functionalities may be immediately required.

Another aspect integral to loading shared libraries involves dealing with versioning and updates. Shared libraries are often updated with new features, performance improvements, or security patches. The dynamic linker must handle these updates gracefully, loading the appropriate version of a library that an application was designed to work with. To manage such scenarios, developers often use versioning schemes and symbol versioning, which allows multiple versions of the same library to coexist on the system. This ensures that applications do not break due to incompatibility with newly released versions.

In addition to the mechanics of loading shared libraries, developers can influence runtime behavior through various environment variables. For instance, the LD_LIBRARY_PATH variable can be set to include additional directories where the dynamic linker should search for shared libraries. Using this variable allows developers and system administrators to test new libraries without altering the system-wide configuration. Other variables, like `LD_PRELOAD`, provide hooks for injecting custom shared libraries before the standard libraries, which is particularly useful for debugging or altering behavior without modifying application binaries.

In conclusion, loading shared libraries at runtime is an intricate, yet elegant aspect of the Linux ecosystem that provides great flexibility and efficiency for software applications. By allowing executables to rely on shared libraries dynamically, developers can create lightweight applications that are easier to maintain and update. As shared libraries become increasingly integral to application architectures, understanding their loading processes, dependencies, and configuration options will empower developers to design more robust, efficient, and modern software solutions that can adapt to changing requirements and environments. Embracing the powerful mechanisms behind runtime library loading is essential for any developer engaging with the evolving landscape of Linux software development.

6. Exploring Linker Tools in Linux

6.1. Overview of Linker Tools

Linker tools in the Linux environment are essential for the process of converting source code into executable programs. These tools assist developers by providing a range of functionalities to manage how code is linked and integrated, streamlining the software development process. The following section offers insights into the key tools employed in linking, focusing on their capabilities and how they fit into the broader context of application development.

One of the most critical tools for linking in Linux is the GNU linker, commonly referred to as `ld`. The GNU linker is the primary linking tool used in the GNU operating system and provides a robust suite of features for combining object files and libraries into a single executable. It handles various linking tasks, including symbol resolution, relocation, and managing dynamic shared libraries. By understanding how to leverage the GNU linker, developers can customize the linking process to suit their application's needs, optimize memory usage, and ensure that all necessary libraries are available during execution. Configuring flags and options in linker commands can significantly affect how the final binary performs.

Another valuable tool for developers is `ldd`, which is used to print shared library dependencies. This tool is instrumental for diagnosing issues related to dynamic libraries, such as dependency resolution failures or missing libraries during runtime. By running `ldd` on an executable, developers can readily see all shared libraries that the application depends on, along with their corresponding paths. This visibility is crucial for troubleshooting and ensures that all necessary components are present for the application to run smoothly. With `ldd`, developers can also ensure compatibility between the executables and the libraries they require.

In addition to `ld` and `ldd`, the `objdump` tool provides techniques for inspecting and analyzing object files and libraries. Developers can use `objdump` to disassemble binary files and examine their contents, which is invaluable for debugging and understanding how code is compiled and linked. For example, the -c option allows for viewing assembly code while the -t option lets developers see symbol tables. By using these functionalities, developers can verify that symbols are correctly linked and can identify potential issues with the linking process. Further, objdump can help in optimizing the code by providing insights into how functions are laid out and whether there are opportunities for reducing overhead or improving execution speed.

Collectively, these linker tools represent just a subset of the extensive toolkit available to developers within the Linux environment. By mastering these tools, developers greatly enhance their capabilities in managing libraries, resolving dependencies, and ensuring the overall efficiency and reliability of the applications they build. The effective use of linker tools becomes especially crucial in complex projects where multiple libraries and dependencies are involved, allowing for streamlined development workflows and improved application performance. As developers familiarize themselves with these tools, they can take full advantage of the dynamic capabilities of the Linux environment, leading to robust and high-performance software solutions.

6.2. ld: The GNU Linker

The GNU Linker, known as 'ld', is an integral tool within the Linux ecosystem that facilitates the linking process of compiling source code into executables. It serves as a bridge between object files created by compilers and the final output that systems can execute. The GNU Linker is often used in conjunction with package managers and build systems, enhancing the process of managing libraries and ensuring that applications run efficiently.

At its core, the GNU Linker performs several vital functions: symbol resolution, relocation, and library management. When an application is compiled, the compiler generates object files that may contain references to functions or variables defined in other files or libraries. The role of the linker is to resolve these references and ensure that the symbols in the object files point to the correct memory addresses in the executable. This process requires the linker to scan through the accompanying libraries, matching symbols from the application with the corresponding definitions in those libraries.

Relocation is another crucial function performed by the GNU Linker. Object files often contain code designed to run at a specific memory address, which is not predetermined during the compilation. During linking, the GNU Linker adjusts these addresses so they are suitable for the final executable. This adjustment ensures that when the application is loaded into memory, all code and data sections are correctly positioned, allowing for seamless execution.

The GNU Linker also provides robust support for handling both static and dynamic libraries. When it comes to static linking, the linker incorporates the necessary library functions directly into the executable, resulting in larger but self-contained application binaries. Conversely, dynamic linking allows applications to call functions from shared libraries stored separately from the executable. This approach leads to reduced executable size and allows for easier updates to the library without requiring the recompilation of dependent applications.

An essential feature of the GNU Linker is its flexibility, which is facilitated by linker scripts. These scripts enable developers to fine-tune the linking process by specifying how various sections of code and libraries should be arranged in memory. For instance, a developer can instruct the linker to place certain functions in specific memory locations, ensuring that they adhere to the constraints of the target environment. This capability is especially crucial in embedded systems and applications with stringent memory requirements.

Using the GNU Linker typically involves executing commands in the terminal. A standard invocation may look like this:

```
ld -o output_executable file1.o file2.o -lsome_library
```

In this command, `-o output_executable` specifies the name of the final executable file, while `file1.o` and `file2.o` are the object files to be linked. The `-l` option followed by a library name indicates to the linker that it should include the corresponding shared library. When using libraries, the linker will search for them in standard system directories unless specified otherwise by the -L option, which allows developers to direct the linker to custom library paths.

The versatility of the GNU Linker extends beyond traditional applications; it can be integrated into various build systems, such as Makefiles and CMake, which automate the compilation and linking process. By embedding linker commands within these systems, developers can efficiently manage large projects with minimal manual intervention.

For debugging and analysis, the GNU Linker is often paired with additional tools such as objdump, which provides insights into the object files and their contents. Using objdump, developers can inspect symbol tables, disassemble code, or verify the arrangement of sections in the object files. The reliance on these supplementary tools allows developers to ensure that the linking process correctly reflects the intended architecture of their applications.

As software development continues to grow more complex, the importance of effective linking cannot be overstated. The GNU Linker is a foundational component of this process, empowering developers to construct reliable, efficient applications while managing dependencies and optimizing performance. Understanding the capabilities and nuances of the GNU Linker equips developers with the knowledge necessary to navigate the intricate landscape of linking in the Linux ecosystem.

6.3. ldd: Print Shared Library Dependencies

The ldd command, short for "list dynamic dependencies," is an essential tool for developers and system administrators working in Linux environments. Its core purpose is to display the shared library dependencies of dynamically linked executable files, thereby enabling users to diagnose potential linking issues and better manage library dependencies.

Using ldd is straightforward. When you run the command followed by the name of an executable file, it outputs a list of shared libraries that the executable depends on, including their respective paths. For instance, if you have an executable named my_application, you can type:

```
ldd my_application
```

The command will print an output similar to the following:

```
linux-vdso.so.1 =>  (0x00007fffa8dff000)
libm.so.6   =>   /lib/x86_64-linux-gnu/libm.so.6
(0x00007fffa8c78000)
libc.so.6   =>   /lib/x86_64-linux-gnu/libc.so.6
(0x00007fffa8c20000)
/lib64/ld-linux-x86-64.so.2 (0x00007fffa8ead000)
```

In this output, each line corresponds to a shared library that the executable is linked against. The left column displays the library name, while the right column shows the path to the library file in the filesystem. Furthermore, ldd also indicates whether any dependencies are missing, which can be particularly vital for troubleshooting runtime issues.

One of the primary benefits of using ldd is its ability to help developers identify missing libraries. When a required shared library is not found, ldd will alert the user by returning a "not found" message next to the library in question. This capability is crucial when deploying applications across different environments, as there may be discrepancies in library availability depending on the system configuration. Identifying these issues early on can help developers address them before they impact the application at runtime.

Additionally, ldd can be used to understand library versions and dependencies. In Linux, shared libraries can exist in multiple versions, and it is vital to ensure that the correct version is referenced by the executable. For instance, if an application was designed to run with libm.so.6 version 2.27, but the system only has version 2.26 installed, it can cause compatibility problems. By using ldd, developers can quickly verify versioning and ensure that the correct library paths are being used.

Moreover, ldd should also be employed for performance analysis. Since the loading of shared libraries can impact the startup time of an application, understanding which libraries are being loaded and how often can help developers optimize their software. Any unnecessary dependencies can be identified and potentially eliminated, leading to leaner and faster applications.

Although ldd provides a wealth of valuable information, it is essential to handle its output with care. In some scenarios, particularly when dealing with applications that rely on plugins or dynamically loaded modules, the output may not capture all dependencies needed at runtime—only those that are linked at compile time. Developers should supplement their use of ldd with additional profiling and debugging tools to gain a comprehensive understanding of all runtime dependencies.

Furthermore, when using ldd, one must be cautious of potential security risks. Since ldd operates by invoking the dynamic linker, executables that have not been sufficiently vetted should be examined carefully to avoid invoking malicious libraries inadvertently. Tools such as strace can be used alongside ldd to monitor system calls that the executable makes when it runs, providing insights into how dependencies are managed during actual execution.

In summary, ldd is a powerful and indispensable tool for managing shared library dependencies in Linux. It allows developers to diagnose linking issues, identify missing libraries, verify version compatibility, and optimize performance by understanding dependency structures. By regularly utilizing ldd throughout the development and deployment processes, developers can ensure that their applications operate correctly across varied environments while taking full advantage of the efficiencies afforded by dynamic linking.

6.4. Using objdump in Library Analysis

In the realm of library analysis within Linux environments, `objdump` stands out as an indispensable tool for developers seeking to understand, optimize, and troubleshoot static and dynamic libraries. This utility provides a wealth of information about object files, executables, and libraries, encompassing a range of functionalities useful for in-depth analysis.

One of the primary uses of `objdump` is to examine the contents of binary files produced during the compilation process. By using the command `objdump -d <file>`, developers can disassemble the file, revealing the assembly language representation of the included machine code. This feature is particularly beneficial for debugging and performance tuning because it allows developers to see how high-level code translates into low-level instructions. The disassembled output gives insights into function calls, control flow, and can help identify sections of code that may be causing bottlenecks or unexpected behavior.

In addition to disassembly, `objdump` provides a multitude of options to analyze various aspects of object files and libraries. Using the -t option reveals the symbol table of the binary, which lists all the symbols (functions and variables) defined or referenced within the file. This information is vital for understanding which functions are being used and can help in identifying any unresolved symbols that might indicate linking problems. When analyzing libraries, developers can look into specific symbols and their associations with other code pieces to verify correct linking.

Moreover, `objdump` can assist in verifying the architecture compatibility of a library. By executing `objdump -f <file>`, developers can obtain information about the file's architecture, ensuring that the compiled binary matches the target system's specifications. For example, recognizing whether a library is compiled for 32-bit or 64-bit architecture is crucial in preventing runtime errors due to mismatched configurations.

In terms of dynamic libraries, analyzing the linkage and dependencies is paramount. The -p option enables users to view headers and sections for a given file, offering insights into which shared libraries are linked with the executable. This analysis can reveal crucial aspects such as versioning information, which can help developers ascertain whether the correct versions of required libraries are installed in the environment.

Furthermore, in cases where functions from libraries are not being utilized when expected, using objdump in conjunction with other tools like nm can illuminate the issue. While nm lists symbols from object files and libraries, objdump gives a more structured view of how these symbols are utilized within the application. Comparing outputs can help in isolating issues related to symbol visibility or ensuring that the linked libraries are indeed providing the expected functions.

The complexity of linking often leads to various problems, such as "missing references" at runtime. When faced with such issues, objdump assists developers in identifying where functions are defined, allowing them to verify if they are included in the expected libraries or if they must investigate additional files. The combined analysis of both associated object files and libraries can streamline the debugging process.

Another powerful feature of objdump is its ability to help in understanding optimizations performed by the compiler. By analyzing the disassembled output alongside the generated assembly code, developers can evaluate how compiler flags and options impact the translated code. This understanding enables effective tuning for optimization strategies, ensuring performance enhancements in both library and application development.

Results from objdump can be saved and compared over time, serving as part of a workflow to monitor changes within a library as it evolves. This change tracking can reveal how updates to libraries affect application performance or behavior, highlighting potential regressions or improvements.

Overall, objdump is a multifaceted tool that significantly aids in library analysis within Linux. Through its capabilities to disassemble code, display symbol tables, analyze architecture compatibility, and inspect dynamic linking details, objdump provides developers with the necessary insights to optimize performance and ensure proper functionality of their applications. Mastery of `objdump` and its options can empower developers in navigating, analyzing, and refining their work with libraries, ensuring efficient and robust software solutions in the Linux ecosystem. This deeper understanding of library mechanisms enables professionals to enhance their software development practices, contribute effectively to collaborative projects, and maintain high standards of quality in their coding efforts.

7. Advanced Techniques for Linking

7.1. Linker Scripts

Linker scripts are an essential tool in the Linux programming ecosystem, providing developers with the power to customize the linking process to meet specific application requirements. By defining how object files and libraries should be arranged in memory during the linking phase, linker scripts can optimize performance, manage memory usage, and ensure that executables are built according to the precise specifications needed for your application.

A linker script is essentially a text file that contains commands and directives that the linker interprets when creating an executable or shared library. In its simplest form, the script specifies the layout of sections, addresses, and alignment requirements, among other options. Here's an overview of how to effectively use linker scripts to customize the linking process.

The basic structure of a linker script consists of various sections that define the memory layout and specific characteristics for how different segments of your code and libraries should be linked together. For example, a typical linker script may have sections for .text, .data, and .bss, which correspond to executable code, initialized data, and uninitialized data, respectively. The following is a basic example of a linker script:

```
SECTIONS {
    . = 0x10000; /* Set the starting address */
    .text : {
        *(.text) /* All text sections from input files */
    }
    .data : {
        *(.data)
    }
    .bss : {
        *(COMMON)
        *(.bss)
    }
}
```

This script instructs the linker to start placing the executable code at the memory address 0x10000, followed by the data and BSS sections. By using expressions like *(*.section) you can specify that the linker should include all sections that match these patterns from all input files, providing great flexibility in handling multiple object files.

A critical feature of linker scripts is the ability to control the addresses where sections are placed. This capability is particularly useful in embedded systems or other contexts where you need deterministic memory layouts. For instance, by defining section addresses, developers can ensure that critical memory areas are reserved for specific functions or data structures, which is crucial in real-time applications where timing and resource constraints are stringent.

Moreover, linker scripts allow for memory management beyond simple layout definitions. You can define regions of memory for specific purposes, such as separating application code from firmware or defining different memory types for different sections. For example:

```
MEMORY {
    RAM (rw) : ORIGIN = 0x20000000, LENGTH = 20K
    FLASH (rx) : ORIGIN = 0x08000000, LENGTH = 128K
}
```

In this case, developers create two memory regions, RAM and FLASH, with specified permissions (read/write and read/execute). This level of control allows for more efficient use of available memory and aids in maintaining data integrity, something that is vital in safety-critical applications.

Linker scripts also support conditional directives, enabling developers to manage differences in linking behavior based on the presence of specific files or configurations. This can be particularly useful in projects that are built for different target architectures or conditions, allowing for variations in how code is linked without modifying the core logic. For instance:

```
\#ifdef USE_FEATURE_X
    .text : {
```

```
      *(.feature_x)
  }
\#endif
```

Incorporating additional sections based on flags or macros helps maintain code cleanliness and adaptability, making it easier to build applications for various deployment scenarios seamlessly.

When developing complex applications, maintaining organization within the linker script is crucial. Developers should ensure comments and logical structuring are utilized in their scripts to facilitate readability. Well-documented linker scripts will significantly aid debugging processes and collaboration within development teams.

Creating a linker script typically involves several steps, from determining the memory layout required by your application to defining the sections, specifying alignments, and ultimately integrating the script into the build process. Most build systems such as Makefiles or CMake can be easily configured to include linker scripts as part of the compilation process, and their application is often as simple as specifying the script with the linker command:

```
gcc -o myapp myapp.o -T my_linker_script.ld
```

This command uses -T to indicate the linker script being utilized. Following that, developers can compile and link their application as specified by the script, resulting in a binary that adheres to their design requirements.

In summary, linker scripts provide developers with an invaluable tool for customizing the linking process in Linux. Through precise control over memory layouts, addresses, section management, and conditional directives, linker scripts can help achieve optimized performance and meet the unique constraints imposed by specific application requirements. As the complexity of software applications continues to grow, mastering linker scripts will become increasingly important for developers striving to create efficient, maintainable software solutions that leverage the full capabilities of the Linux environment.

7.2. Optimizing the Linker Process

Optimizing the linker process is a fundamental technique in enhancing the efficiency of application development and building robust executables in Linux environments. This subchapter delves into various strategies that developers can employ to streamline the linking process, reduce compile times, and ultimately improve both resource management and performance.

One primary method of optimizing the linker process is through the use of linker scripts. A linker script allows developers to define how object files and libraries should be organized in memory during the linking phase. By controlling section placement, alignment, and memory layout, developers can ensure that their applications use memory efficiently. For instance, developers can arrange critical functions in specific memory regions to enhance cache coherence, ultimately leading to faster execution times.

Implementing versioning strategies also plays a crucial role in the optimization of the linker process. By properly managing versioning for shared libraries and ensuring that executables dynamically link to the appropriate versions, developers can reduce the overhead associated with symbol resolution at startup. Utilizing tools like ldd to check dependencies and version compatibility can preempt runtime errors and mitigate the need for frequent recompilation.

Moreover, organizing code into smaller, more manageable components is essential for optimizations. By segmenting application logic into distinct modules, developers can reduce linking times as the linker can process smaller object files instead of large monolithic binaries. This modular approach not only speeds up the linking process but also enhances code maintainability and facilitates parallel development by allowing different teams to work on separate modules concurrently.

Another notable optimization technique is leveraging link-time code generation (LTCG). LTCG is a powerful approach that enables the compiler to optimize across translation units. When compiling with link-time optimizations enabled, the compiler can analyze the entire program's structure. This deep analysis allows it to eliminate unused functions, inline critical functions, and reorganize code for optimal performance, resulting in a more efficient and smaller final executable.

Incorporating precompiled headers can greatly improve compile times and, by extension, the linking process. Precompiled headers store the compiled representation of commonly used header files, helping to minimize the number of files that need to be processed with each compilation. Reducing the amount of code that the linker must handle during each building cycle not only accelerates the course of each build but also mitigates the overall development time.

Another essential aspect of linking optimization is managing library dependencies. Developers should aim to minimize the number of dependencies their applications introduce. Each additional dependency can lead to longer linking times and increased complexity during deployment. Using static analysis tools to identify unused or redundant libraries and optimizing them can significantly reduce the linking workload.

Parallel linking offers another way to optimize the process. Most modern build systems can utilize multiple cores or threads to perform linking operations. Enabling parallel linking allows the linker to resolve symbols and manage multiple object files simultaneously, reducing the time it takes to complete the linking phase. This strategy is particularly beneficial in large-scale projects with numerous modules and dependencies.

Lastly, utilizing build automation tools like Makefiles, CMake, or Ninja can streamline the build and linking processes. These tools can manage dependencies automatically, track changes, and execute only the necessary compilation and linking steps when changes are detected. By automating the building and linking steps, developers can avoid manual errors and reduce the likelihood of unnecessary recompilation.

In conclusion, optimizing the linker process is pivotal for enhancing both development and application performance in Linux environments. Through strategies like utilizing flexible linker scripts, implementing versioning, modularizing code, leveraging link-time optimizations, using precompiled headers, minimizing dependencies, enabling parallel processing, and utilizing build automation tools, developers can significantly improve their linking processes. By adopting these practices, they can ensure that their applications are not only efficient but also readily maintainable, setting the stage for successful software development and deployment.

7.3. Cross Compilation and Linking

Linking in software development is a complex process, particularly when dealing with cross-compilation and linking across different system architectures. Cross-compilation involves compiling software intended for one platform (target) while running on a different platform (host). As Linux environments span a diverse range of devices, from embedded systems to high-performance servers, mastering cross-compilation and linking is essential for developers aiming to create reliable applications that perform optimally across various systems.

The first challenge in cross-compilation is ensuring that the correct cross-compiler is utilized. A cross-compiler generates executable code for a different architecture than the one it is running on. Developers must install cross-compilers that correspond to the target architecture. For instance, if one is aiming to compile a program for an ARM-based embedded device while developing on an x86 host machine, the developer needs to install an ARM cross-compiler, such as `gcc-arm-linux-gnueabi`. This deviation can require a specific setup where the developer has to adjust their build environment to explicitly utilize this toolchain.

Once the appropriate cross-compiler is in place, developers face the task of addressing the dependencies and libraries tailored for the target architecture. Dynamic and static libraries must be available in versions compiled for the target architecture, substantially complicating the linking process. The challenge arises when libraries contain architecture-specific code, and simply linking libraries built for x86 will likely yield undefined behavior or runtime crashes on an ARM device. Developers can avoid this issue by utilizing a sysroot—a directory containing a full filesystem layout of the target system, including necessary libraries and headers.

When linking during cross-compilation, the linker must also be properly directed to the architecture-specific library paths. This can involve setting environment variables such as `LIBRARY_PATH` and `C_INCLUDE_PATH` to point to directories within the sysroot, ensuring the correct libraries are found during the linking stage. Additionally, for dynamic libraries, developers should ensure that the `rpath` or `runpath` sections are correctly configured to enable the application to locate its required libraries at runtime, maintaining correct reference paths back to the library versions for the target architecture.

Alongside these technical intricacies, developers should also consider the performance implications of their linking choices in a cross-compilation context. Inline assembly or architecture-specific optimizations can yield significant performance improvements, but these often necessitate separate builds for each platform. Developers must create build scripts to facilitate the management of these distinct builds, typically employing build systems like CMake or Autoconf, which support cross-compilation configurations through toolchain files. By defining different build configurations within these systems, developers can streamline the process of building and linking code for multiple architectures.

Moreover, testing becomes another critical aspect of cross-compilation and linking. Unit tests and integration tests need to be run on the target device rather than the host environment to ascertain that all linked libraries work seamlessly in the actual deployment scenario. Consequently, using emulators or hardware simulation along with continuous integration practices can significantly enhance testing efficiency by automating the build and deployment process to the target architecture.

Debugging in cross-compilation scenarios presents unique challenges as well. It often involves cross-debugging tools, such as gdb with remote debugging capabilities, which can connect to the target device or virtual machine. This allows developers to analyze the behavior of their applications in their original environment while still deploying and compiling from their development machine.

In summary, cross-compilation and linking present an array of challenges stemming from the need for appropriate toolchains, system libraries, and careful management of dependencies across different architectures. Emphasizing a clear build and linking strategy, developers must ensure that they configure their environment properly to accommodate the nuances of cross-compiling while optimizing for performance, correctness, and maintainability. The landscape of cross-compilation in Linux is multifaceted, but with the right approach, developers can create versatile applications that function seamlessly across a wide array of devices and platforms.

7.4. Link-time Code Generation and Optimization

Link-time code generation (LTCG) and optimization are advanced techniques that enhance the performance of software programs during the linking phase of application development. These practices enable compilers and linkers to analyze and optimize code at a higher level, leading to more efficient executables. This subchapter focuses on the core concepts, methodologies, benefits, challenges, and tools associated with link-time code generation and optimization, providing a comprehensive overview of their relevance in modern Linux development.

Link-time code generation allows for optimizations that span across multiple translation units (source files). Unlike traditional compilation, wherein each translation unit is compiled independently, LTCG analyzes the entire program context during the linking process. This holistic view of the program allows the compiler to make more informed optimization decisions, resulting in improved performance and reduced resource consumption. The underlying goal of LTCG is to enable optimizations that cannot be achieved when compilation occurs in isolation.

One significant advantage of LTCG is the opportunity to eliminate dead code. When a program is compiled separately, it may include references to functions that are not used, leading to an increase in the executable size and unnecessary memory usage. With link-time analysis, the compiler can identify which functions and variables are actually utilized by the program and exclude those that are not. This leads to smaller executables that load faster and consume less memory, a critical factor in resource-constrained environments and applications where performance is paramount.

Function inlining is another beneficial optimization achievable with LTCG. This technique allows the compiler to replace function calls with the actual body of the function, reducing the overhead associated with function calls such as argument passing and jumping to another code segment. This can result in more efficient execution of frequently called functions and enhance overall performance, particularly in compute-intensive applications such as numerical computations or graphics rendering.

Additionally, LTCG can enable interprocedural optimizations, allowing the compiler to analyze and optimize across function calls. By examining how functions interact with one another, the compiler can reorder instructions for better locality of reference and cache utilization. This enhances execution speed as the likelihood of cache hits increases, leading to reduced memory access latency. Such optimization is particularly beneficial in applications with complex function hierarchies and significant interdependencies.

Compiler flags and options play a vital role in determining whether link-time code generation is applied. Developers can enable these optimizations during the build process by using specific flags. For instance, in GCC, the `-flto` flag activates link-time optimization, allowing the compiler to perform these advanced analyses and optimizations during the linking stage.

However, while LTCG offers substantial advantages, it also introduces certain challenges. The compilation and linking process may become more complex, as it requires a deeper integration between the compiler and linker. Each build must account for the time-consuming nature of link-time optimizations, leading to increased overall build times, especially in large projects. To mitigate this, developers often strike a balance between the level of optimization and build time, selectively applying LTCG to performance-critical parts of the codebase and maintaining development convenience during iterations.

Another challenge lies in managing dependencies between translation units. As interdependencies become more complex, changes to a single translation unit may necessitate a complete recompilation of the entire program to maintain optimization benefits. Developers must therefore carefully balance the need for fine-grained optimizations with the impact on build workflows and revision control.

Tools and methodologies have emerged to facilitate link-time code generation in Linux environments. For instance, modern build systems such as CMake and Meson are increasingly incorporating support for LTCG, helping developers easily configure their projects for link-time optimization. Additionally, continuous integration (CI) pipelines can integrate LTCG as part of automated builds, ensuring optimized versions of code are automatically generated, tested, and deployed.

Profiling tools also play a crucial role in understanding where LTCG can be effectively applied. Tools such as gprof and perf can analyze execution characteristics, highlighting frequently executed functions that may benefit from inlining or other optimizations offered by link-time code generation. By analyzing performance profiles, developers can make informed decisions on where to focus optimization efforts.

In summary, link-time code generation and optimization serve as powerful techniques for enhancing software performance in Linux development. By allowing compilers to analyze and optimize the entire program context at the linking phase, developers can achieve significant reductions in executable size, improved runtime performance, and optimized memory usage. Despite the inherent challenges in adopting these techniques, the benefits they confer make them a critical aspect of modern software development practices. Understanding and effectively implementing LTCG can empower developers to create high-performance applications capable of meeting the demands of today's fast-paced computing environments.

8. System Library Management

8.1. The Role of Package Managers

The role of package managers in managing Linux libraries cannot be overstated. These sophisticated tools streamline the installation, upgrading, configuration, and removal of software packages, and they play a crucial role in controlling and organizing system libraries to ensure that applications can run smoothly and efficiently.

At their core, package managers automate the process of managing software installations and dependencies. When developers create applications, they often rely on various libraries to provide essential functionalities. However, these libraries may have their own dependencies, leading to a complex web of interrelated components that need to be addressed. Package managers help developers and system administrators resolve these dependencies automatically, ensuring that all necessary libraries are installed in the correct versions without manual intervention.

There are two primary types of package managers commonly used in Linux distributions: those that manage software using binary packages (such as APT for Debian-based systems and RPM for Red Hat-based systems) and those designed for source packages (such as Gentoo's Portage). The choice of package manager often depends on the Linux distribution, which is tailored for specific use-cases and user experience.

One key aspect of package managers is their ability to track which packages are installed on the system, along with their versions. This tracking is essential for effective library management. If a library is updated, for instance, the package manager can identify all applications that depend on that library, allowing users to assess the impact of the update. If version conflicts arise—say, if one application requires an older version of a library while another demands a newer version —the package manager can help manage these scenarios effectively, either by providing different versions of the same library or by alerting the system administrator to the conflict.

Additionally, package managers facilitate the integration of software updates and security patches. Regularly updating libraries is critical to maintaining the security and stability of applications. Most package managers come equipped with repository support, allowing them to pull the latest versions of libraries and packages efficiently. Users can easily check for available updates and apply them as necessary, reducing the window of exposure to potential vulnerabilities.

When it comes to library conflicts, package managers provide a variety of powerful solutions. They can manage different versions of libraries by using namespace techniques or by allowing the installation of parallel versions of libraries. For example, developers might use "libfoo.so.1" for one application and "libfoo.so.2" for another to resolve issues of overlapping library names. Package managers will typically maintain detailed metadata about these different versions, enabling the system to load the appropriate libraries dynamically based on which application requests them.

Furthermore, package managers often include resources for dependency resolution, which ensures that libraries are installed in the order required for their successful operation. This prevents scenarios in which an application fails to start because it cannot locate a dependent library.

Another important role played by package managers is that of dependency management during the installation of new software. For instance, when a user attempts to install an application that requires a specific library, the package manager automatically identifies the required library and any of its dependencies, retrieving and installing them seamlessly. This functionality is particularly beneficial in minimizing "dependency hell," a common scenario in which recursive dependencies between libraries can lead to confusion and installation failures.

Package managers also enhance collaboration within the developer community by supporting repositories that host libraries and applications. Package maintainers can submit their libraries to repository managers, enhancing the overall ecosystem by allowing users to discover and install high-quality software more easily. This also contributes to the overall reliability and security of the software, as it provides a single source of truth for library versions and their compatibility with various applications.

Furthermore, many package managers enable the creation of custom repositories, which can be useful for organizations that have specific library requirements or wish to host their internal tools. In such cases, the package manager facilitates the packaging and deployment of libraries into a controlled environment, ensuring that developers access the correct versions.

In conclusion, the role of package managers in Linux library management is paramount. They streamline the process of installing, updating, and managing software libraries, ensuring that applications run reliably and efficiently. By automating dependency resolution, tracking library versions, managing conflicts, and integrating security updates, package managers are indispensable tools in the developer and system administrator's toolkit. Understanding and utilizing the capabilities of package managers is essential for anyone involved in Linux software development, as they enhance productivity, system stability, and security across the board. With their ongoing evolution and integration into modern development practices, mastering package management is a key skill facilitated by the Linux ecosystem.

8.2. Dealing with Library Conflicts

Handling library conflicts is a fundamental aspect of software development and system maintenance within Linux environments. With the proliferation of libraries and continuous improvements in software design practices, conflicts can arise when multiple applications rely on different versions of the same library or when shared libraries have overlapping dependencies. Addressing these conflicts efficiently is crucial for ensuring application stability, minimizing downtime, and maintaining robust system performance.

One of the foremost strategies for dealing with library conflicts is thorough dependency management. Developers must maintain a clear understanding of the libraries their applications depend on and the versions required by each component. This often involves utilizing a package manager, such as APT or RPM, which automates the installation and management of library dependencies. By using package managers, users can avoid manual errors commonly associated with library installations and ensure that they satisfy all dependency requirements effectively.

Moreover, maintaining good documentation regarding library versions, compatibility, and usage is essential. Documentation provides a comprehensive reference guide for developers and system administrators to troubleshoot conflicts when they arise. By adopting rigorous versioning practices, such as semantic versioning, teams can better communicate the nature of changes in libraries and their potential impact on dependent applications, reducing the likelihood of conflicts.

Another effective maneuver is the use of containerization technologies like Docker. Containers bundle up applications with their dependencies, ensuring that each application runs with its specific library versions in self-contained environments. This isolation makes it significantly easier to run multiple applications that may require different versions of the same library without interference. By leveraging containerization, organizations can deploy applications with minimal risk of library conflicts on shared environments.

Additionally, developers can mitigate library conflicts through 'Namespace' techniques, particularly in the context of dynamic libraries. Namespacing allows multiple versions of the same library to coexist simultaneously without overriding each other. For instance, by managing installation paths, developers can specify which version of a library should be used based on the application context. This capability allows for greater flexibility and ensures that applications remain stable, even when libraries are required to diverge.

Library path configurations also play a pivotal role in addressing conflicts. The LD_LIBRARY_PATH environment variable in Linux can be used to specify locations of libraries manually, allowing individual applications to reference specific directories. By controlling the search path for libraries, developers can prioritize particular versions that are compatible with their applications. However, while this method can be beneficial, it should be used judiciously to avoid issues related to library version collisions.

When existing libraries conflict, it is essential to consider compiling custom versions. Developers can create static libraries or build forked versions of libraries tailored for specific applications. This approach allows applications to avoid dependence on the system-wide libraries and use customized versions, helping avoid conflicts altogether. However, care must be taken to manage updates to these custom builds to incorporate security patches and optimizations.

Utilizing tools like ldd can aid in detecting library dependencies before application execution. By checking which libraries an executable needs prior to running it, developers can foresee potential conflicts and remedy them before they cause runtime issues. Such proactive measures can significantly reduce application downtime and ensure smoother deployment cycles.

Furthermore, many development teams adopt Continuous Integration (CI) and Continuous Deployment (CD) practices to streamline library management and conflict resolution. By running automated tests before deploying applications, CI/CD pipelines can verify that the correct library versions are in place and that there are no pending dependencies that could lead to conflicts. This process helps catch errors as early as possible, minimizing the chances of conflicts slipping into production systems.

It's also critical to establish a culture of caution around library updates in shared environments. Whenever a library is updated, the potential implications for all dependent applications must be assessed to ensure the changes don't introduce new conflicts. The roll-back procedures should be well defined and documented, allowing teams to revert to previous library versions if newly introduced changes create instability.

Lastly, community engagement and open-source support can offer rich resources for resolving library conflicts. Engaging with the broader developer community through forums, documentation, and collaborative tools like GitHub can provide insights into common issues and solutions others have found effective. Many libraries within the Linux ecosystem also maintain active channels for reporting issues, suggesting improvements, and sharing best practices, enabling organization-wide learning and adaptation.

In conclusion, dealing with library conflicts in Linux systems requires a multifaceted strategy that encompasses thorough dependency management, using containerization technologies, maintaining clear documentation, employing namespace techniques, and leveraging tools for proactive detection. By establishing robust processes, engaging with the community, and adhering to best practices, developers and system administrators can effectively manage library conflicts, ensuring the stability and reliability of their applications.

8.3. Updating and Maintaining Libraries

As software development in Linux environments continues to evolve, so does the importance of updating and maintaining libraries. Libraries are foundational components of applications, providing reusable code that enhances efficiency and functionality. However, with these benefits come the obligations associated with ensuring libraries are up-to-date and secure. This subchapter explores the best practices for managing libraries, mitigating vulnerabilities, and ensuring that applications continue to function optimally in a dynamic ecosystem.

One of the foremost practices is establishing a routine for updating libraries. Regularly checking for updates to libraries ensures that applications benefit from the latest features, optimizations, and security patches. Open-source libraries, in particular, tend to have active communities that release updates often; hence, staying informed about these releases is crucial. Developers can utilize tools like package managers to automate this process, allowing for seamless integration of updates into the existing systems. Tools like `apt`, `yum`, or `pacman` can be configured to check for updates regularly and notify developers or users about available library upgrades.

Another significant aspect of maintaining libraries is managing dependencies. Applications often rely on a network of interdependent libraries, and it's essential to track these dependencies meticulously. Dependency management tools, such as `pip` for Python or `npm` for Node.js, can simplify this task by providing tools for version control and conflict resolution. Ensuring that the correct versions of libraries are always used, especially when multiple applications share the same dependencies, minimizes the risk of encountering runtime issues due to version mismatches.

Security vulnerabilities are a primary concern regarding library maintenance. Libraries, particularly those sourced from third parties, may contain undiscovered vulnerabilities that can expose applications to security risks. To mitigate this, employing security audits and vulnerability scanning tools can significantly enhance an application's security posture. Tools like `Clair`, which analyze container images for known vulnerabilities, or `Snyk`, which provides security insights into dependencies, can help identify issues before they manifest in production. Additionally, following security advisories from library maintainers and subscribing to vulnerability databases can assist developers in staying informed about potential threats.

Moreover, adopting a proactive approach to vulnerability management is critical. Creating a policy for immediate action when a vulnerability report is issued—such as deploying patches, updating libraries, or even temporarily disabling affected components—can prevent exploitation in live environments. Every developer should have a protocol in place for emergency updates, reducing time to mitigate processes, and ensuring that remediation happens swiftly and effectively.

In addition to regular updates, documentation is vital for maintaining libraries. Properly documenting library usage, configurations, and versioning helps in understanding implications when updates occur. Clear documentation aids both current and future team members in grasping the context of library usage within the application. Using tools to generate documentation automatically based on comments and code structures can simplify this process and ensure it remains current as changes are made.

Automating tests for application functionality after library updates is another critical practice. Continuous Integration/Continuous Deployment (CI/CD) processes should include automated testing frameworks that verify the compatibility of the application with updated libraries. Unit tests, integration tests, and user acceptance tests should be routinely executed post-update to catch any discrepancies caused by library changes. Having a robust testing pipeline ensures that the application retains its expected performance and functionality despite the evolving library landscape.

Furthermore, using Version Control Systems (VCS) can enhance the management of library changes. When a library is updated, it should be tracked within the VCS, allowing developers to roll back changes if unforeseen problems arise. This enables a form of versioning for libraries within your application and ensures that developers have access to previous working states.

Managing the lifecycle of libraries also involves understanding how libraries interact with operational and deployment environments. For instance, containerization technologies like Docker can help isolate libraries and minimize the risks of conflicts arising from shared environments. Moreover, containers can encapsulate the version of libraries together with the application, ensuring that deployments are reproducible and stable across development, testing, and production environments.

In summary, effective updating and maintaining of libraries in Linux development hinge on several best practices: regular updates, dependency management, vulnerability assessments, thorough documentation, automated testing, version control, and strategic use of modern deployment technologies. Adopting these practices will not only enhance security and functionality but also empower developers to build robust, maintainable applications capable of adapting to the intricate ecosystem of Linux libraries. By prioritizing library management, developers can ensure that their applications remain efficient, reliable, and secure in a rapidly changing technological landscape.

8.4. Security Considerations in Libraries

In the realm of software development, libraries are essential components of applications, providing reusable code and functionalities that enhance productivity and efficiency. However, with the integration of libraries comes the need for a comprehensive understanding of security considerations, particularly in the context of libraries in Linux. As cyber threats continue to evolve, it is crucial for developers and system administrators to adopt best practices that safeguard libraries from vulnerabilities and attacks.

One of the fundamental aspects of securing libraries is ensuring that they are kept up to date. Libraries often receive patches and updates from their maintainers to address security vulnerabilities. Regularly updating libraries reduces the risk of exploitation from known vulnerabilities. Developers should implement processes to monitor the libraries being used in their applications and allocate time for regular updates. This can be accomplished through the use of package managers, which automate the process of checking for and installing library updates.

Another consideration is the evaluation of third-party libraries. Using external libraries can introduce risks if they are not sourced from reputable repositories or maintained by trustworthy authors. Developers should conduct thorough assessments of third-party libraries, reviewing their codebases for security vulnerabilities, compliance with licensing terms, and community support. Tools such as static analysis can help identify potential risks within the library code itself.

Furthermore, the principles of least privilege should be applied when granting access to libraries and their associated binaries. Developers should minimize the permissions assigned to the libraries, ensuring that they only have the access necessary to function correctly. This principle limits the potential damage that can be inflicted in the event of a library compromise.

Implementing security measures such as Address Space Layout Randomization (ASLR) can further enhance the protection of libraries. ASLR randomizes the memory addresses assigned to library functions, making it more difficult for attackers to predict where their payloads should be injected. By utilizing ASLR, developers can make it significantly harder for malicious actors to exploit vulnerabilities within libraries.

Dynamic libraries add an additional layer of complexity when it comes to security considerations. The use of shared libraries can expose applications to risks if the libraries are compromised or replaced with malicious versions. To mitigate this risk, developers should consider implementing integrity checks to verify that shared libraries have not been tampered with, either through digital signatures or hashing methods.

Another strategy to enhance security is to enforce the separation of concerns. By designing applications such that different functionalities are encapsulated within separate libraries, the overall attack surface can be minimized. In this manner, if one library is compromised, it does not automatically jeopardize the entire application, isolating the risk and allowing for more straightforward remediation.

Logging and monitoring library usage is another effective approach to maintain security. Implementing logging mechanisms to track library usage and any anomalous behavior can help in incident detection and response. Monitoring should include tracking the versions of libraries in use and any updates applied. If an unexpected library version is detected, alerts can be triggered for further investigation.

Developers should also educate themselves and their teams about secure coding practices specific to libraries. This includes understanding how to handle data passed to libraries securely and validating input parameters against buffer overflows and injections. By adopting secure coding techniques, developers can minimize the chances of introducing vulnerabilities into their libraries.

In addition to addressing security at the library level, a broader understanding of collaboration with the community is vital. Engaging with other developers through forums, release notes, and security advisories can keep teams aware of potential vulnerabilities and best practices when using and managing libraries. The open-source community is particularly useful in this regard, as it often shares information and tools aimed at enhancing library security.

In summary, the security considerations within libraries in Linux are multifaceted and require careful attention throughout the software development lifecycle. By establishing processes for regular updates, evaluating third-party libraries diligently, applying the principles of least privilege, utilizing security measures like ASLR, separating functionalities, monitoring usage, and fostering collaboration with the community, developers and system administrators can significantly enhance the security posture of applications that rely on various libraries. The importance of security cannot be overstated, especially as the threats become increasingly sophisticated, solidifying libraries as both critical assets and potential vulnerabilities within the software ecosystem.

9. The Process of Debugging and Testing Linked Applications

9.1. Debugging with GDB

Debugging is an essential part of the software development process, particularly when it comes to linked applications in the Linux environment. In this context, GDB (GNU Debugger) serves as a powerful tool, enabling developers to inspect their applications during execution, identify issues, and understand the behavior of program linked with various libraries. This subchapter delves into the nuances of utilizing GDB for debugging linked applications, guiding users through its features, commands, and best practices.

At its core, GDB allows developers to observe the execution of a program while it is running or during a crash, providing an environment where they can inspect the state of the application, including variable values, call stacks, and memory usage. To get started with debugging a linked application using GDB, the first step is to ensure that the application is compiled with debugging information. This is typically achieved by including the -g option during the compilation phase. For example:

```
gcc -g -o myapp myapp.c -lmylibrary
```

By compiling with -g, GDB can provide detailed context about the program's symbols, functions, and source lines, allowing developers to step through the code as it runs.

Once the application is compiled with debugging information, launching GDB is straightforward. The syntax involves specifying the compiled program you want to debug:

```
gdb ./myapp
```

Upon entering the GDB command line interface, developers can utilize a range of powerful commands to control program execution. One of the most fundamental commands is run, which starts executing the

81

specified program. If the application takes command-line arguments, these can be passed directly after the run command. For example:

```
(gdb) run arg1 arg2
```

If the program encounters a crash or generates a segmentation fault, GDB will halt execution and display the location of the error, providing insights into the problematic code. At this point, developers can use the command backtrace, abbreviated as bt, to view the call stack leading to the crash. This information is critical for diagnosing how the program reached its current state.

GDB also supports setting breakpoints, which are specific locations in the code where execution will pause. This allows developers to examine variables and control flow before proceeding. Breakpoints can be set using the break command, specifying either a function name or a line number:

```
(gdb) break main
(gdb) break myapp.c:25
```

Once a breakpoint is reached, execution can be resumed using the continue command, or the state of the program can be inspected with commands such as print. For example, print variable_name will display the current value of a specified variable, which can be particularly useful for diagnosing logic errors or verifying that data is being passed correctly between functions.

Additionally, GDB excels at handling multi-threaded applications, enabling developers to switch between different threads to inspect their individual states. By utilizing the info threads command, developers can view a list of all threads and switch between them with thread thread_number. Understanding how different threads interact with each other and libraries they share is vital for diagnosing concurrency issues or deadlocks.

When debugging linked applications, memory inspection is another crucial aspect. The x command in GDB is used to examine memory addresses in various formats, providing visibility into structures, arrays, and raw memory blocks. For instance, x/10x &myvariable would display the memory at the address of myvariable in hexadecimal format.

GDB also supports remote debugging over a network connection, facilitating the debugging of applications running on different machines or embedded systems. This is achieved by using GDBserver, which listens for commands from the GDB instance on the development machine. This approach is invaluable when working with applications in embedded environments, where direct access to hardware may not be possible.

As with any complex tool, mastering GDB requires practice and patience. It is advisable for developers to familiarize themselves with the comprehensive GDB manual, which includes detailed descriptions of commands, options, and examples. Leveraging additional resources like community forums, video tutorials, and documentation can also enhance one's proficiency in effective debugging practices.

In conclusion, GDB is an indispensable tool for debugging linked applications in Linux, providing developers with a suite of features that facilitate deep inspection of applications, control over execution flow, and analysis of memory usage. By compiling applications with debugging information and utilizing GDB's powerful commands, developers can effectively address issues, understand application behavior, and ensure their software performs reliably in the dynamic context of linked libraries. Implementing GDB into the development workflow can significantly enhance the quality of applications and expedite the debugging process, ultimately leading to more robust and maintainable software solutions.

9.2. Valgrind's Role in Link Efficiency

Valgrind is a powerful suite of debugging and profiling tools that plays a crucial role in optimizing link efficiency within Linux applications. Specifically designed to detect memory management issues, such as memory leaks, heap misuse, and uninitialized memory access, Valgrind enables developers to enhance the reliability and performance of linked applications by identifying potential inefficiencies that may arise from their dependencies on libraries.

One of the primary tools in the Valgrind suite is Memcheck, a memory analysis tool that assists in identifying memory-related errors by monitoring how memory is allocated and deallocated during program execution. Memory leaks can occur in any application, especially when it creates dynamic objects but fails to free memory once the objects are no longer needed. In linked applications, where multiple libraries and modules work together seamlessly, the source of a memory leak may not be readily apparent. Valgrind alleviates this issue by providing a detailed report of all memory allocations and deallocations.

To use Valgrind with a linked application, developers typically run the executable under Valgrind's control using a command like:

```
valgrind --leak-check=full --track-origins=yes ./
my_application
```

The `--leak-check=full` option instructs Valgrind to conduct an exhaustive analysis of memory leaks, while `--track-origins=yes` helps pinpoint where uninitialized values originated. This depth of analysis allows developers to pinpoint not only that a leak has occurred but also where in the code it can be tracked, making it significantly easier to address.

Valgrind's output includes information about each memory allocation, detailing the location in the code where memory management errors occurred. For example, developers can see stack traces for memory leaks or invalid memory accesses, allowing for direct correlation with the corresponding sections of source code. This targeted diagnosis is indispensable when working with complex systems that incorporate multiple linked libraries, as it often takes a focused analysis to uncover how different components interact or fail to deallocate memory properly.

In addition to detection of memory leaks, Valgrind can also be instrumental in improving performance through its "cachegrind" tool, which analyzes cache usage patterns. Linked applications sometimes suffer performance penalties from inefficient memory usage or suboptimal access patterns in shared libraries. By running a linked application in cachegrind, developers can obtain a detailed report of cache hits and misses, cache line usage, and instruction counts. This information is particularly useful for optimizing critical sections of code and ensuring that the interactions between libraries and the main application do not lead to bottlenecks.

When a cachegrind report is generated, developers can use visualization tools like `kcachegrind` to visually interpret the data, making it easier to identify performance hotspots. By correlating resource usage metrics with specific libraries, developers can focus their optimization efforts precisely where they will bring the most significant performance benefits.

In a landscape where software must frequently adapt to changes in libraries and applications, Valgrind aids in maintaining link efficiency. During development, integrating Valgrind checks into continuous integration (CI) workflows can help ensure that any changes made to libraries or application code do not inadvertently introduce memory inefficiencies. Automating these checks provides ongoing assurance of application stability and efficiency, even as linked components evolve.

Furthermore, Valgrind supports a variety of output options and logging mechanisms, allowing developers to customize their analysis. For instance, developers can focus on specific modules of a large application or create suppression files to filter known issues that are not relevant to their current testing focus, streamlining their debugging workflow.

Valgrind is particularly beneficial in large, complex applications, where understanding the interactions of multiple libraries can pose a challenge. By highlighting memory allocation patterns and validating efficient usage of shared libraries, it offers insights that can lead to more effective linking practices and informed architectural decisions.

Another important community aspect of Valgrind is its active development and user engagement. Developers modifying or creating their own libraries can contribute to Valgrind's ecosystem by ensuring their libraries work seamlessly within the Valgrind environment. This symbiotic relationship can lead to broader recognition of issues across libraries and share insights into common memory management pitfalls faced in linked applications.

In conclusion, Valgrind serves as an invaluable tool for ensuring link efficiency in Linux applications. By facilitating the detection of memory leaks, tracking memory usage patterns, and providing insights into cache performance, Valgrind empowers developers to enhance code reliability and performance. Integrating Valgrind into the development and CI workflow enables proactive management of memory-related issues, ultimately contributing to the creation of robust applications that leverage the full potential of linked libraries while maintaining optimal performance.

9.3. Automated Testing Techniques

Automated Testing Techniques encompass a critical range of practices and tools that significantly enhance the reliability and robustness of software applications, particularly those that involve complex linking scenarios in Linux environments. Automated testing refers to the use of software tools to execute tests on code automatically, ensuring that the application behaves as expected in various conditions without requiring manual intervention. These techniques are especially vital when working with linked applications, where multiple components and libraries interact in intricate ways, leading to potential points of failure.

One of the primary automated testing techniques involves unit testing, where individual functions or components of a program are tested in isolation. This method allows developers to validate the smallest parts of their application, ensuring that each function behaves correctly. In the context of linked applications, unit tests can help identify issues within specific library functions. Frameworks such as Google Test for C++ or PyTest for Python facilitate the creation and execution of unit tests, allowing developers to run comprehensive test suites quickly. The automated nature of these frameworks means that every time changes are made to the codebase or libraries, tests can be executed to catch regressions or new bugs efficiently.

Integration testing is another vital technique in the automated testing landscape. It focuses on verifying that different modules and libraries work together as intended. In linked applications, where multiple components are tied together, integration tests can help ensure that the interactions between libraries do not introduce new issues. Automated tools like Jenkins or Travis CI can be configured to run integration tests as part of a continuous integration (CI) pipeline, executing these tests each time new code is added or existing code is modified. This process is crucial in identifying discrepancies between how components interact and ensuring stable integration points.

For systems that rely heavily on user interaction, automated testing can extend to functional testing, where the entire application is tested against user requirements and specifications. Tools like Selenium and Cypress are particularly useful for web applications, allowing developers to simulate user interactions and verify that the application responds correctly. In linked applications, it is essential to ensure that the functionality exposed by different libraries integrates well into the user experience. Automated functional tests help provide confidence that new changes do not disrupt existing workflows.

Another significant aspect of automated testing techniques is regression testing. Through this technique, developers run existing tests whenever modifications are made to confirm that previously working features remain functional. As linked applications evolve—sometimes introducing new libraries or updating existing ones—automated regression tests act as a safety net, automatically verifying feature integrity and reducing the risk of inadvertently breaking functionality due to changes in linked code.

Exploratory testing can also benefit from automation by utilizing tools that simulate various workflows to identify potential edge cases or unknown issues. Although exploratory testing is traditionally a manual process, automation can enhance it by creating dynamic test cases that trigger unexpected user flows. This is particularly beneficial for identifying how changes in one part of the application might cascade into unexpected results elsewhere, especially in systems with multiple linked libraries.

Performance testing is yet another area where automated techniques are crucial. Ensuring that a linked application performs efficiently under various load conditions can be challenging. Tools like Apache JMeter or Gatling can be employed to automate performance testing, providing valuable insights into how different components respond under stress. By simulating various load scenarios, developers can pinpoint performance bottlenecks, particularly in interactions between libraries.

Security testing also warrants attention within automated testing techniques. Tools such as OWASP ZAP or Burp Suite can perform automated security testing on linked applications, identifying vulnerabilities that could arise from incorrect handling of libraries or insecure dependencies. Automated scans can help catch issues before they reach production, enforcing best practices for secure linking and handling of libraries.

Furthermore, incorporating automated testing tools into a CI/CD pipeline fosters a culture of continuous quality. As part of the development workflow, these tools facilitate regular execution of tests whenever changes are made, ensuring that linked applications maintain reliability and performance. This shift from manual testing to automated processes allows teams to respond swiftly to issues and continuously improve their software quality.

In conclusion, automated testing techniques play a pivotal role in ensuring the quality and reliability of linked applications in Linux environments. Through unit tests, integration tests, functional tests, regression tests, performance tests, and security tests, developers can comprehensively validate their applications with efficiency and speed. Leveraging automation not only enhances the testing process but also supports a culture of continuous integration and delivery, ultimately leading to more robust software solutions that leverage complex linking strategies effectively. By implementing these automated testing practices, developers can safeguard their applications against bugs and performance issues, paving the way for successful outcomes in sophisticated software projects.

9.4. Address Sanitizer Testing

Address Sanitizer (ASan) testing is a critical process for identifying memory-related issues in applications, particularly those that are linked with multiple libraries in the complex ecosystem of Linux. ASan is designed to catch memory corruption errors such as buffer overflows, use-after-free errors, and memory leaks, which can be rampant in any non-trivial application relying on dynamic and static libraries. As such, its relevance extends across various types of applications, from single-module utilities to large-scale systems utilizing intricate linking practices. This chapter will explore the principles of Address Sanitizer testing, its integration into the development workflow, and the practical steps involved in utilizing ASan effectively.

Address Sanitizer is a fast memory error detector provided as part of the LLVM and GCC compilers. By instrumenting the code at compile time, ASan adds additional data structures that track memory usage and valid pointers, enabling runtime checks during the execution of the program. One of its standout features is its ability to offer detailed reports about memory access violations, including the location of the erroneous access and the stack trace at the time of the error. This functionality is invaluable for developers as it significantly simplifies the debugging process, allowing them to locate and resolve issues quickly.

The integration of ASan into the development cycle is straightforward. In order to utilize ASan, developers need to compile their applications with specific flags to enable address sanitizer diagnostics. For instance, they can use the following command:

```
gcc -fsanitize=address -g -o my_application
my_application.c -lmylibrary
```

With the -fsanitize=address flag, ASan is enabled for the compiled code, and the -g option ensures that debugging information is available, facilitating easy navigation in error reports.

Once the application has been compiled with ASan support, developers can run their application as normal. If any memory corruption issues arise during execution, ASan will intercept these violations and print an error message to the console, detailing the nature of the error. For example, a typical output might look like:

```
==12345==ERROR: AddressSanitizer: heap-buffer-overflow on
address 0x60200000a10 at pc 0x49c630 bp 0x7ffd5d3fb970 sp
0x7ffd5d3fb968
READ of size 4 at 0x60200000a10 thread T0
    \#0 0x49c62f in function_name /path/to/source.c:10
    \#1 0x49d7e1 in main /path/to/source.c:20
```

In this output, the developer is informed about the type of error (heap-buffer-overflow), the address where it occurred, the size of the offending operation, and the call stack, including the specific file and line number. This level of granularity directly supports efficient troubleshooting.

For linked applications, ASan's detailed reporting becomes even more crucial. Memory corruption issues may not stem directly from the application code but might arise from interactions with external libraries. Consequently, thorough testing with ASan can help pinpoint the exact source of memory misuse, whether it derives from the application or a dependent library. When testing an application that connects to several libraries, particularly when these libraries have been developed by different teams or sourced externally, the importance of ASan is magnified. Developers can uncover subtle interactions that may lead to corruption without ASan's instrumentation, which would otherwise be very challenging to diagnose.

Another advantage of ASan is its ability to detect memory leaks. When memory is allocated but not properly released, relying on memory analysis tools such as Valgrind can be resource-intensive. ASan provides an immediate and convenient diagnostic option that is fast and integrates well into the development process. Developers can run their application and simply check the ASan output for any reports of leaked memory.

In addition to basic usage, ASan has various options to customize its behavior. For example, developers can use the `-fsanitizer-coverage=trace` option to collect additional coverage data. This detailed information can help in understanding how different parts of the application interact with libraries, providing insight into which functions are invoked frequently and where potential inefficiencies lie.

Despite its advantages, there are considerations developers must be aware of when utilizing ASan. One of the limitations is performance overhead, as the instrumentation added to the code can slow executions, usually around a factor of 2-3 times compared to the uninstrumented version. As ASan is primarily intended for testing and debugging rather than production use, its overhead is generally acceptable in a testing context.

Additionally, certain configurations can lead to incompatibilities with other sanitizers or debugging tools, so understanding the limitations of the environment set up is essential. For instance, ASan and certain multithreading libraries might lead to errors if not handled properly. Developers should refer to the documentation to understand how to configure ASan optimally alongside other tools they may wish to incorporate in their development workflows.

In summary, Address Sanitizer testing provides a powerful mechanism for identifying memory-related issues in linked applications within the Linux environment. By integrating ASan into the development process, developers can quickly catch and diagnose memory corruption errors, leading to enhanced reliability and robustness in their software systems. Coupled with its complementary capabilities in leak detection, ASan stands out as an invaluable tool for modern software development, driving towards improved quality in applications that rely on complex linking and interdependent libraries. By prioritizing such methodologies, development teams can significantly reduce the incidence of memory-related failures and improve the stability of their applications before reaching production environments.

10. Case Studies in Linux Linking

10.1. Linking in Large Scale Applications

Linking in large-scale applications is a critical aspect of software engineering that involves integrating multiple libraries and modules to create a cohesive and functional software product. Understanding the intricacies of linking in this context is essential for managing complex dependencies, maintaining performance, and ensuring reliability across the software application lifecycle.

In large-scale applications, developers often work with numerous libraries—some of which may be part of the application's codebase, while others are third-party or open-source libraries. Each library may provide essential functions or services, and it's the responsibility of the linker to coordinate how these libraries interact with one another and how they are included in the final executable.

One of the key challenges in linking large-scale applications is managing dependencies. As the number of dependencies grows, the complexity increases exponentially. Developers need to ensure that the right versions of libraries are present in the environment where the application will run. Inconsistent library versions can lead to "dependency hell," where applications fail to execute due to conflicting requirements. To mitigate this issue, developers can employ dependency management tools, such as package managers (e.g., APT, RPM), which automate the process of notifying users of available updates and managing library versions.

To streamline the linking process, it is often beneficial to adopt modular programming practices. By organizing code into microservices or separate modules, developers can build applications that are easier to maintain, test, and update. Each module can interface with specific libraries, thus isolating changes and minimizing the impact on the overall application. This approach not only simplifies the linking process but also enhances code reuse, allowing common functionalities to be shared across different projects.

Consider the example of a large-scale web application that relies on multiple services such as user authentication, payment processing, and data storage. Each of these services may have its own library requirements. Instead of directly linking each library to the main application, the developers can create service-oriented architecture (SOA). Each service can operate independently with its respective libraries. The main application interacts with these services through well-defined APIs, reducing the need for direct linking and simplifying the overall architecture.

At the linker level, optimization is another critical consideration in large-scale applications. Linkers can employ various strategies to optimize resource usage and application performance. For example, using link-time optimization (LTO) allows the compiler to analyze entire programs and make optimizations that span across different modules. This leads to more efficient binaries that can execute faster and consume fewer resources.

Dynamic loading and linking are also beneficial strategies in large-scale applications. By enabling the application to load libraries at runtime, developers can reduce the initial startup time of the application. This feature allows applications to load only the libraries they need while running, leading to more efficient memory management. Additionally, if a library is updated, the application does not need to be recompiled; it can simply use the latest version of the library when it restarts.

Testing and debugging linked libraries in large-scale applications necessitate robust practices. Tools such as GDB (GNU Debugger) and Valgrind are instrumental in identifying issues such as memory leaks and segmentation faults. Implementing comprehensive unit and integration tests in conjunction with continuous integration/continuous deployment (CI/CD) pipelines allows development teams to promptly catch regressions as they merge new code or update existing libraries.

Furthermore, in large systems, logging and monitoring become essential for lifecycle management. Recording library loads, performance metrics, and error messages provides valuable insights into how libraries are behaving in production. This data can subsequently inform decisions about library updates, refactoring code, or even replacing underperforming libraries.

Security is another significant concern when dealing with large-scale applications and linking. Vulnerabilities in one library can affect all dependent applications. Regular audits, updates, and the implementation of secure coding practices are paramount. Moreover, employing tools such as Dependency-Check can be beneficial in proactive scanning for known vulnerabilities in the libraries used, fostering a culture of security from the ground up.

In conclusion, linking in large-scale applications requires a thoughtful and systematic approach to managing libraries and dependencies. By adopting modular architectures, leveraging tools for optimization, implementing robust testing frameworks, and paying careful attention to security concerns, developers can create resilient applications that effectively harness the power of linked libraries. Understanding these practices is essential for anyone involved in the development, maintenance, or expansion of large-scale software systems in the Linux ecosystem.

10.2. Small but Mighty: Linking in Lightweight Applications

In modern software development, particularly within the Linux ecosystem, the practice of linking lightweight applications is both an art and a necessity. The ability to create small, efficient applications that leverage libraries effectively is critical in a world that increasingly prioritizes speed, resource efficiency, and maintainability. While traditional linking practices are well-documented for larger applications, the subtleties and strategies for lightweight applications warrant a focused exploration.

Lightweight applications often stand out due to their reduced footprint, making them ideal for environments where resource constraints are common, such as embedded systems or mobile devices.

However, the benefits of linking can extend across a range of applications designed to minimize overhead, from command-line utilities to microservices deployed in cloud environments.

A crucial aspect to consider in linking lightweight applications is the selection of appropriate libraries. In a lightweight context, it is imperative to avoid hefty libraries that may bloat the application size or introduce unnecessary functionality. Developers must critically evaluate library dependencies, opting for minimalistic libraries that provide only the required functionalities. For instance, rather than relying on a comprehensive library that offers hundreds of functions, one might choose a specialized library that targets only the necessary tasks. This selective approach not only reduces the size of the binary but can also optimize execution time, as there is less overhead incurred from calling unnecessary code.

Beyond the selection of libraries, developers should focus on optimizing the way libraries are integrated within the application during the linking process. This can involve utilizing static linking for small-scale applications where deployment simplicity is favored over runtime flexibility. By statically linking libraries, developers ensure that all required code is incorporated into a single executable, making the distribution simpler, particularly in environments where managing dynamic library dependencies can be cumbersome.

However, developers must also recognize the trade-offs associated with static linking. While it removes runtime dependencies and can simplify deployments, it can also lead to larger executable sizes and the necessity to recompile the application for any updates in the libraries used. To mitigate this, a hybrid approach, wherein selectively static links are made with certain libraries while others are linked dynamically, may be employed. This could ensure that the core functionalities remain lightweight, while components that may require frequent updates can benefit from the flexibility offered by dynamic linking.

Another essential strategy involves the thoughtful design of the application's architecture itself. Lightweight applications should be designed with modularity in mind, allowing components to be linked dynamically when needed. Techniques such as service-oriented architecture (SOA) enable libraries to be encapsulated within individual services. By decoupling functionalities into microservices, the main application can remain lightweight, only contracting the services it needs at any given time. This not only lowers the memory footprint but also makes the application easier to maintain since individual services can be updated or replaced without impacting the core application.

The way library imports are handled also matters. Utilizing lazy loading techniques allows applications to defer the loading of unnecessary libraries until they are explicitly required. This approach conserves memory and minimizes initial startup time, which is particularly valuable in environments where quick responsiveness is vital.

Performance considerations are paramount in lightweight linking, so it is advantageous to employ profiling tools to analyze the performance of linked applications. Profiling enables developers to understand how linked libraries interact in real-time, allowing for targeted optimizations. Developers can utilize tools like `gprof` or `perf` to gain insights into function call frequencies and execution times, identifying any bottlenecks caused by library interactions.

As libraries evolve and developers must frequently deal with updates and patches, automating library management can prove beneficial. Package managers like `apt` or `yum` can be leveraged to ensure that lightweight applications are always running against the latest versions of their libraries without introducing unnecessary complexity in the application itself.

In conclusion, linking strategies for lightweight applications in the Linux environment focus on resource efficiency, modular design, and targeted library selection. By critically evaluating library dependencies, streamlining integration techniques, employing profiling tools, and maintaining modularity throughout application design, developers can harness the benefits of linking to create responsive, efficient applications that stand up to modern demands. Understanding these strategies is essential for anyone looking to excel in developing lightweight software solutions within the Linux ecosystem, ultimately paving the way for innovation in usability and performance.

10.3. Ecosystem Linking Patterns

In the ecosystem of Linux linking, patterns of interaction and behavior between libraries, applications, and the linker itself emerge as crucial factors that shape the way systems operate. These ecosystem linking patterns not only dictate how applications are built, maintained, and optimized but also serve as a foundation for best practices that enhance software resilience, efficiency, and adaptability over time. Understanding these patterns enables developers and system architects to design better applications that utilize the full potential of libraries, leading to improved performance and reliability.

One of the most significant linking patterns that has established itself in the Linux ecosystem revolves around dependency management. In an environment where numerous applications and libraries interact, developers often face challenges related to versioning and compatibility. Utilizing package managers has become the norm to streamline dependency resolution. Package managers such as APT, YUM, or Pacman help manage library installations, ensuring that applications have access to the correct versions of dependencies required for their smooth operation. The use of these tools has become commonplace, creating a standardized way of handling dependencies that developers can rely on.

Another prevalent linking pattern is the adoption of modular programming practices. The principle of separating code into distinct modules or libraries allows for greater abstraction and reuse, making it easier for developers to manage codebases, test components in isolation, and dynamically link modules as needed. This pattern promotes a more flexible coding environment, where applications can evolve by simply updating individual libraries without requiring extensive rewrites of code. The emergence of microservices and service-oriented architectures has further accelerated this trend, breaking applications into smaller, independently deployable services that communicate over APIs, thus simplifying the linking process.

The dynamic nature of linking patterns in the Linux ecosystem also manifests in the increasing use of runtime loading and linking techniques. This trend emphasizes the need for applications to load libraries on-demand, only when they are required during execution. Techniques like dynamic linking allow libraries to remain separate from the application binaries, reducing the overall executable size and providing a more modular approach that facilitates easier updates. This flexibility is essential in environments where applications need to adapt quickly to changes without incurring long downtimes traditionally associated with static linking.

Performance optimization remains a core focus within the ecosystem linking patterns. Linkers now routinely incorporate optimizations such as link-time optimization (LTO) that leverages whole-program analysis to produce more efficient output. This pattern reflects a shift towards integrating performance considerations within the linking phase rather than treating it as a discrete final step in the build process. Developers are increasingly adopting profiling tools alongside linking, allowing them to make informed decisions based on usage metrics and performance bottlenecks gathered during the execution of applications.

Security considerations also influence ecosystem linking patterns. With vulnerabilities discovered regularly in widely used libraries, the linking process now incorporates security practices such as static and dynamic analysis of libraries before linking them into applications. The implementation of tools that scan for known vulnerabilities ensures that developers are aware of risks associated with the libraries they choose to link against. This pattern of proactive security assessment is becoming integral to the software development lifecycle as organizations strive to create secure applications.

Moreover, community-driven developments and open-source contributions have resulted in an evolving landscape of linking patterns. As developers share libraries and innovations, established best practices emerge, guiding newer developers in implementing effective linking strategies. Platforms such as GitHub enable collaboration and facilitate the sharing of libraries tailored for specific functions, further enriching the ecosystem. The community becomes a critical driver for adopting and refining linking patterns, resulting in a vibrant ecosystem responsive to developers' needs.

However, failures in linking do offer valuable lessons learned. In this ecosystem, the analysis of past linking failures often highlights common pitfalls developers encounter. Mismanaged dependencies, improper versioning, and misleading documentation are often leading causes of linking failures. Reflecting on these past mistakes can guide developers to establish better practices in dependency management, implement proper testing strategies, and enhance communication within development teams.

In conclusion, the ecosystem linking patterns within Linux represent a dynamic interplay of strategies and methods that developers utilize to create efficient, modular, and secure applications. By recognizing and understanding these patterns—dependency management practices, modular programming, runtime loading techniques, performance optimization, and security considerations—developers are better equipped to design robust applications that can adapt and thrive in the ever-changing landscape of software development. Furthermore, learning from the past while actively engaging with the community positions developers and organizations to capitalize on future innovations in linking strategies and methodologies.

10.4. Learning from Mistakes: Linking Failures

Learning from mistakes is crucial in the realm of software development, especially when it comes to linking in Linux. The failures encountered during the linking process can provide invaluable lessons that shape future practices and prevent recurrence. Analyzing past linking failures helps developers adopt a proactive approach, enhancing both their understanding of underlying mechanisms and their capability to respond to challenges effectively.

One of the most common mistakes in linking is a failure to properly manage library dependencies. In large applications, where numerous components from different libraries are interconnected, developers may overlook specific version requirements or the presence of conflicts between libraries. Such oversights can result in runtime errors that may be difficult to diagnose. Learning from these mistakes involves implementing better dependency management practices, utilizing tools such as package managers that automate the installation of libraries while ensuring version compatibility. By establishing robust processes to track and manage dependencies, developers can mitigate the risk of runtime issues stemming from improper linking.

In some instances, static linking can also lead to failures when applications are compiled with outdated library versions or different configurations. An example of this is when an application relying on a statically linked library needs to be updated, but the compilation process does not take into account changes in the library's API. Here, the lesson to learn is about the importance of maintaining versioning protocols and clear documentation. When modifying or updating libraries, developers should ensure that they maintain backward compatibility, or clearly communicate any breaking changes to all dependent applications.

Another notable failure can arise from improper use of dynamic linking. Developers might over-rely on dynamically linked libraries without appropriately managing their versions and availability, resulting in applications malfunctioning if a necessary library is inadvertently removed or updated. This scenario highlights the need for diligent monitoring of library dependencies, especially in production environments. Developers should establish routines to regularly check for updates on shared libraries, implementing alerts for any significant changes that could affect application functionality.

Security vulnerabilities also serve as critical learning points in linking failures. A common pitfall arises from the use of third-party libraries with known vulnerabilities that may not be swiftly updated. Such instances can expose applications to significant risks. From this, the takeaway is clear: developers must prioritize security reviews of all external libraries utilized within their applications. Conducting regular security audits and using tools to scan for known vulnerabilities can prevent linking errors that stem from insecure libraries. Having a defined policy for handling security-related library updates can enhance application security and reduce the chances of exploitation.

Moreover, the lessons learned from documentation failures cannot be understated. Many linking mistakes occur due to insufficient or unclear documentation regarding library usage or integration procedures. Consequently, developers may struggle to understand the requirements and intricate relationships between libraries. Emphasizing a culture of thorough documentation—detailing library versions, dependencies, setup instructions, and behavior—can significantly improve the onboarding process for new team members and ensure smoother workflows during development.

Testing practices also present opportunities for learning from linking failures. Often, insufficient testing can lead to serious issues going unnoticed until they manifest in production. Developers should embrace automated testing frameworks that verify the integration and functionality of linked libraries. Comprehensive test suites, including unit tests, integration tests, and end-to-end tests, can provide critical insights into how libraries interact and ensure that new changes do not introduce regressions. Emphasizing a "fail-fast" approach—where problems are identified early through rigorous testing—can be pivotal in detecting linking issues before they become problematic.

Lastly, when examining broader industry trends, some linking failures may highlight the need to adapt best practices over time. For instance, as containers and microservices gain increased adoption, traditional linking practices may not suffice in these new paradigms. Learning to establish container-friendly linking strategies that emphasize isolation and minimal dependencies can contribute to more resilient software designs.

In conclusion, linking failures in Linux offer significant learning opportunities that can inform and enhance future development practices. By focusing on dependency management, version control, security vigilance, robust documentation, rigorous testing protocols, and adaptability in emerging trends, developers can mitigate risks and build more robust linking strategies. Embracing the experiences derived from failures not only aids in refining technical skills but also cultivates a culture of continuous improvement among development teams. As the landscape of software development evolves, leveraging lessons learned from past mistakes ensures that both individuals and organizations can thrive in the dynamic world of Linux linking.

11. Future of Linking in Linux

11.1. Emerging Trends and Technologies

In the fast-evolving landscape of software development, particularly within the Linux ecosystem, emerging trends and technologies continually reshape how developers approach the linking process. As applications grow in complexity, an understanding of these trends becomes increasingly paramount for programmers seeking to optimize their software solutions. The future of linking in Linux will be influenced by advancements across various dimensions, including automation, containerization, performance optimization, and community-driven innovations, all of which drive toward creating more efficient, maintainable, and secure applications.

One of the most significant emerging trends is the increased adoption of automation in the build and linking processes. Tools such as Continuous Integration (CI) and Continuous Deployment (CD) are becoming ubiquitous, enabling developers to automate the testing and deployment of applications. As a result, practices that ensure consistent library versions, systematic dependency management, and automated testing cycles will become essential components of the linking process. Developers will increasingly rely on automated scripts and tools that facilitate the linking of code across various environments, consistencies, and requirements, thereby minimizing human error while enhancing productivity.

The growing trend of containerization also significantly impacts linking strategies in Linux applications. Container orchestration platforms, like Docker and Kubernetes, emphasize microservices architectures, where lightweight applications are distributed across various nodes with specific library dependencies. This trend necessitates a reevaluation of traditional linking methods and requires developers to devise strategies that minimize image sizes while ensuring dynamic dependencies are efficiently managed. As containerization continues to gain popularity, developers will need to adopt linking practices that incorporate the principles of isolation, scalability, and adaptability to thrive in diverse deployment environments.

Performance optimization remains a pivotal focus in linking technologies. With applications increasingly required to handle large volumes of data and simultaneous user interactions, developers will seek ways to optimize memory usage, execution speed, and startup times. Innovations like Just-In-Time (JIT) compilation and link-time optimization (LTO) will become more mainstream, allowing compilers to optimize across translation units. As organizations aim for performance gains, understanding the implications of linking on execution efficiency will be paramount. Developers who can harness advanced optimization techniques during the linking phase will certainly provide a competitive edge in developing performance-critical applications.

Security also looms large in the future of linking technologies. As vulnerabilities in libraries and the dependencies they create continue to be exposed, secure linking practices will be paramount. Real-time security assessments and validation tools will evolve, enabling developers to automatically assess libraries for vulnerabilities and dynamically link to updated secure versions. Furthermore, building security into the linking process will encourage the adoption of proactive measures such as monitoring library changes and relying on established community practices to fortify against exploitation.

The developer community plays a crucial role in the evolution of linking practices. Open-source contributions and collaborative frameworks promote continuous improvement and innovation among developers. Platforms like GitHub not only facilitate the sharing of libraries but also serve as spaces for open discussions about best practices in linking, offering an avenue for community members to collectively identify common challenges and propose solutions. As developers engage with and contribute to the community, they foster a more robust ecosystem that enhances the overall capabilities of linking technologies in Linux.

In summary, the future of linking in Linux will witness the convergence of automation, containerization, ongoing performance optimization, and heightened security measures. These emerging trends and technologies will redefine how linking is approached, shaping the development landscape towards more efficient, scalable, and secure applications. By keeping an eye on these trends, developers can equip themselves with the knowledge necessary to stay relevant and take full advantage of the technologies and methodologies that will drive the future of software development in the Linux ecosystem.

11.2. Innovations on the Horizon

Innovations on the Horizon

As we look ahead to the future of linking within the Linux ecosystem, several potential innovations are poised to redefine how developers approach the linking process. These advancements could stem from emerging technologies, evolving practices, and community-driven efforts aimed at enhancing the efficiency, flexibility, and security of library integration in software applications.

One of the most promising areas of innovation is the integration of artificial intelligence (AI) and machine learning in dependency management and linking processes. By harnessing AI to analyze project characteristics, library usage patterns, and historical data, developers could receive intelligent recommendations on library versions, potential conflicts, and optimal linking strategies. This predictive capability could help minimize linking errors and ensure that applications remain stable and up-to-date, significantly reducing the overhead associated with library management.

In tandem with AI integration, the trend towards more sophisticated package management systems is expected to continue. The evolution of these systems could facilitate better version control, improved dependency resolution algorithms, and seamless handling of library updates. Future package managers may incorporate advanced analytics that allow for real-time monitoring of library vulnerabilities and alerts as new versions are released, automatically suggesting or applying updates as needed. This proactive approach to library maintenance could yield enhanced security and application performance.

Containerization technologies are also likely to influence innovations in linking practices. With the growth of microservices architecture, linking strategies may evolve to streamline how containers handle shared libraries. Future innovations could enable smarter methods for versioning and managing libraries within containerized deployments, allowing developers to encapsulate not only the application code but also its dependencies more effectively. This could include enhanced capabilities for dynamically loading libraries based on service requirements and optimizing resource usage across distributed environments.

Modular application development is another area ripe for innovation. As the movement towards composability and microservices continues, technology designed to facilitate seamless collaboration between numerous interconnected libraries could emerge. This might involve new linking frameworks capable of managing dynamic connections and interactions in real time, allowing libraries to be integrated or replaced on-the-fly without downtime. Such adaptive linking practices would enhance application resilience and responsiveness to changing demands.

The rise of edge computing also opens up new frontiers for linking innovations. As computing resources are distributed closer to the data source and user, the requirements for linking in edge environments differ from traditional cloud-based applications. Future innovations may involve specialized linkers equipped to optimize performance and resource management across diverse and often resource-constrained edge devices, integrating real-time data with existing library functionality while minimizing latency.

Furthermore, the importance of security will continue to shape innovations in library linking. Future advancements may see the development of secure linkage protocols that verify the integrity and authenticity of shared libraries dynamically. Techniques such as blockchain could offer transparent and tamper-proof solutions for managing library versions and dependencies, allowing users to trace the origin and validity of libraries used in their applications. This layer of security would provide developers with greater confidence when using third-party libraries, an essential aspect of linking practices.

In addition to library management and securing linking processes, the role of community engagement and open-source contributions will be essential in driving future innovations. Collaborative efforts can lead to the creation of new best practices, shared learning experiences, and innovative tools that enhance linking methodologies. Hackathons, open-source projects, and community forums can serve as incubators for exploring novel ideas and strategies with real-world applicability, ensuring that the ecosystem remains dynamic and responsive to emerging challenges.

Finally, ongoing research in compiler technologies and optimization techniques will likely yield significant advancements in linking processes. Innovations in just-in-time (JIT) compilation and link-time optimizations can provide unprecedented performance benefits. By optimizing code across modules during the linking stage, applications can run faster and more efficiently while reducing memory overhead. Exciting opportunities await those willing to explore these avant-garde linking concepts as they emerge within the landscape.

In summary, the innovations on the horizon for linking in Linux promise to enhance how developers manage libraries, optimize performance, and secure their applications. By embracing these advancements—fueled by AI, modular architectures, container technologies, edge computing, and community-driven resources—developers can create applications that not only meet current demands but also adapt swiftly to future challenges, ensuring the vitality and relevance of the Linux ecosystem in an ever-evolving landscape.

11.3. Developer Community and Open Source Contributions

In the landscape of software development and systems engineering, the significance of developer communities and open-source contributions cannot be overstated, particularly in the realm of linking in Linux. These collaborative networks serve as vibrant ecosystems where knowledge is exchanged, innovative ideas take shape, and critical advancements in linking methodologies are made. Understanding their role and the impact they have on linking practices enables developers and organizations to leverage community resources effectively, shaping the future of software technology.

At the heart of the developer community lies a shared commitment to open-source principles, which advocate for transparency, collaboration, and the free sharing of knowledge. In the Linux ecosystem, this manifests as myriad libraries, frameworks, and tools available for developers to utilize in their projects. The open-source model enables programmers to contribute back, enhancing libraries through code contributions, documentation, bug reports, and feature requests. This cycle of contribution and improvement fosters continuous innovation, leading to robust linking practices that benefit the entire community.

One significant advantage of participating in developer communities is the collaborative problem-solving environment they provide. Developers often encounter challenges related to linking, such as managing dependencies, ensuring compatibility, or resolving conflicts between libraries. By engaging with peers through forums, mailing lists, and collaborative platforms like GitHub, developers can share experiences and solutions. This collective wisdom enables the community to respond rapidly to emerging issues, facilitating the identification and implementation of best practices in linking strategies.

Open-source contributions have also led to the development of powerful tools that streamline the linking process. Community-driven projects such as CMake, meson, and Bazel have emerged as robust build systems that enable automated and efficient linking, making it easier for developers to manage complicated dependency graphs. These tools evolve with ongoing community input, reflecting a wide array of use cases and enabling customization that caters to diverse project requirements.

Moreover, developer communities offer invaluable educational resources. Tutorials, workshops, and documentation generated by experienced community members help new developers navigate the complexities of linking in Linux. This knowledge sharing is essential for fostering a new generation of engineers who can leverage libraries effectively, contribute back to the community, and push the boundaries of what is possible in software development.

In addition, as the field of software engineering continues to grow, so too does the need for addressing ethical and legal considerations in linking practices. Open-source licenses dictate how libraries can be used, modified, and shared, underscoring the importance of understanding these frameworks within the community. The discourse surrounding these licenses ensures that developers remain informed about legal obligations and ethical responsibilities, promoting responsible and fair usage of community contributions.

Looking toward the future, the vitality of developer communities and their open-source contributions is likely to remain a cornerstone of innovation in linking practices. As new technologies, such as AI-driven development tools and more sophisticated package management systems, emerge, the community will play a critical role in shaping their adoption and implementation. Moreover, as the demand for secure and reliable software increases, collaborative efforts in security reviews and testing will likely become paramount, driving the evolution of linking practices to meet new challenges.

In conclusion, the synergy between developer communities and open-source contributions forms the backbone of progress in linking methodologies within the Linux ecosystem. By participating in and contributing to these communities, developers not only enhance their own skills but also contribute to a collective intelligence that drives innovation and best practices. The ongoing dialogues that emerge from these interactions pave the way for the future of linking in Linux, ensuring that it remains a dynamic and continually improving field reflective of the collaborative spirit inherent in open-source development.

11.4. Predicting Performance Paradigms

In large-scale applications, linking becomes a critical process that directly impacts how components interact and perform. The integration of multiple libraries and modules highlights the importance of efficient linking strategies that can manage complexity while maximizing performance. Application developers must navigate challenges associated with dependencies, ensure compatibility across various libraries, and maintain application reliability.

One of the primary challenges in linking large-scale applications is the management of dependencies. As applications grow and evolve, they often depend on numerous libraries, some of which may have their own dependencies. This complex web of interdependent components can lead to issues like "dependency hell," where conflicting library versions disrupt execution. This is where tools like package managers become indispensable, automating the process of ensuring correct versions are installed and minimizing human error. By utilizing these tools, developers can streamline the management of dependencies, ensuring that their libraries are kept up to date and compatible with their applications.

Building modular applications is a strategy that can mitigate the challenges associated with linking. By decomposing applications into smaller, reusable modules or services, developers can improve the maintainability and scalability of their software. This modular approach allows for a clear separation of concerns, enabling developers to focus on individual components while simplifying the linking process. Each module can encapsulate its dependencies, reducing the complexity involved when linking the entire application.

Dynamic linking also plays a vital role in large-scale applications, allowing libraries to be loaded and linked at runtime rather than compile time. This means that applications can share common libraries, which not only conserves memory but also allows for seamless updates without the need to recompile the entire application. This flexibility is essential in environments where applications must adapt quickly to changes in library versions or patches.

Performance optimization is another critical consideration when linking large-scale applications. Given the potential performance overhead associated with linking—especially as applications scale—developers should utilize tools and techniques designed to assess and enhance performance. Link-time optimization (LTO) is one such technique that allows the compiler to analyze and optimize code across multiple modules during the linking phase. This produces smaller, more efficient binaries that can execute faster and use memory more effectively.

Testing and debugging become more complex in large-scale systems, making it essential to leverage robust frameworks for both unit testing and integration testing. Tools such as GDB (GNU Debugger) and Valgrind can help identify issues within linked libraries, allowing developers to troubleshoot problems effectively. Comprehensive testing strategies are vital to ensure that individual components work harmoniously and do not unintentionally disrupt system functionality.

As the community around Linux and open-source software continues to grow, shared knowledge and best practices for linking in large-scale applications become increasingly accessible. Collaboration through community forums, documentation, and open-source contributions enables developers to share insights and tackle common challenges collectively. The ability to engage with a vast network of like-minded individuals can further enhance developers' capabilities in building robust applications and navigating the complexities of linking.

In conclusion, linking in large-scale applications is a multifaceted process that requires careful management of dependencies, modular design principles, dynamic linking strategies, performance optimization, and rigorous testing practices. By embracing community resources and leveraging automation tools, developers can effectively navigate the challenges of linking in complex applications, ultimately leading to more efficient, maintainable, and reliable software systems that meet the demands of modern computing environments. Understanding these principles will equip developers with the knowledge needed to create robust, high-performance applications in the evolving landscape of Linux software development.

12. Linking in Embedded Systems

12.1. Embedded System Constraints

In an era defined by technology advancement, embedded systems represent a unique intersection of software development and hardware constraints, requiring a nuanced approach to linking libraries and applications. Embedded systems, designed to perform specific tasks within constrained environments, often face stringent limitations in memory, processing power, and energy consumption. This subchapter delves into the critical embedded system constraints that influence how linking is approached in these compact devices.

One of the most significant constraints in embedded systems is limited memory availability. Unlike general-purpose computers, embedded devices typically have finite amounts of RAM and storage. This limitation necessitates a careful balancing act regarding the size of executable files and the libraries that are linked. Developers must prioritize lightweight libraries that merely provide the essential functionality needed for the application. This often involves judicious selection and sometimes even custom coding to ensure that only the necessary code is included, minimizing the footprint of the final binaries.

Memory fragmentation is another challenge associated with embedded systems that can complicate the linking process. Over time, as memory is allocated and deallocated for various tasks, fragmentation can lead to inefficient memory utilization. Static linking can exacerbate fragmentation issues, as the entirety of library code may need to reside in memory even if only a fraction of that code is used. Thus, dynamic linking might seem like a viable option; however, it introduces its challenges—such as the overhead of runtime linking and reliance on an external storage medium that may be slow or limited in embedded contexts.

Power management is another critical constraint in embedded systems that must be accounted for during linking. Many embedded devices operate on battery power and need to maximize energy efficiency. Linking practices that result in high memory usage or prolonged CPU activity can detract from power efficiency, rendering the device less effective for its intended application. To counteract this, developers can implement strategies such as link-time optimization to create as compact binaries as possible, reducing CPU cycles and memory access times during execution. Furthermore, utilizing functional libraries that offer power-efficient algorithms can play a vital role in achieving energy conservation.

Real-time performance requirements impose additional constraints on linking in embedded systems. Many embedded applications demand deterministic behavior, where timing is critical—such as in automotive or medical devices where performance can affect safety. Linking practices must ensure that the runtime path of function calls within libraries can achieve predictable response times, which often calls for an examination of how libraries interact and the latency introduced by linking methods. As the interplay between static and dynamic linking is scrutinized, developers tend to gravitate towards static linking for critical components to avoid latency and ensure that responses occur within expected timeframes.

Debugging linked libraries in embedded environments introduces yet another layer of complexity, as traditional debugging tools may not function adequately in resource-constrained settings. Developers must leverage lightweight debugging tools capable of interfacing with the target hardware effectively. Some sophisticated embedded environments may provide simulators or emulators that can mimic hardware behaviors for testing purposes, allowing developers to test and debug linked library behavior before deployment.

The lack of standardized libraries for specific hardware architectures can also present challenges when developing for embedded systems. Unlike general-purpose libraries, embedded libraries may not have the same rigor in testing or may lack comprehensive documentation, leading to compatibility issues. Developers need to navigate potential barriers when integrating libraries, possibly leading to custom solutions to bridge gaps produced by proprietary components. This reflects the necessity of thorough testing and documentation practices throughout the development lifecycle.

As the internet of things (IoT) continues to proliferate, the constraints surrounding embedded systems will influence future generations of linking practices. The desire for interoperability, low power consumption, and reliability in IoT devices will encourage the adoption of advanced linking methodologies that emphasize modularity, flexibility, and performance optimization. For instance, microservices architectures may extend to the embedded domain, allowing components to communicate seamlessly while reducing memory constraints through shared library calls.

In conclusion, linking in embedded systems is characterized by a delicate balance of constraints including memory limitations, power consumption, real-time performance requirements, debugging challenges, and varying library support. As technology advances, embedding innovative linking strategies that prioritize efficiency and performance will remain critical for developers operating within the constraints of embedded environments. A nuanced approach that adapts to these challenges ensures that applications can effectively leverage libraries while meeting the demands of modern embedded systems, paving the way for smarter and more capable devices.

12.2. Optimizing for Limited Resources

Optimizing for limited resources is an essential strategy in the Linux ecosystem, particularly when dealing with lightweight applications or embedded systems. By maximizing efficiency and minimizing overhead, developers can create applications that perform well while operating under stringent constraints. This section will delve into various practical methods and techniques for optimizing linking processes to ensure the best possible use of limited resources.

First and foremost, understanding the target hardware specifications is crucial. Developers must identify the constraints of the system, such as available memory, processing power, and energy consumption. This understanding allows for informed decisions on which libraries to use, how to structure the application, and what linking techniques to implement. By carefully selecting lightweight, purpose-built libraries, developers can ensure that their applications provide the necessary functionality without unnecessary bloat.

When linking applications, static linking can be beneficial in resource-constrained environments. By embedding libraries directly within the executable, static linking eliminates the need for the application to depend on external dynamic libraries. This approach not only reduces the complexity of the deployment (avoiding the "dependency hell" scenario) but often leads to faster execution times, as the application can directly access all required code without the overhead associated with dynamic linking. However, care must be taken when using static libraries as they can increase executable sizes significantly; therefore, they should be selected judiciously based on application requirements.

Dynamic linking, in contrast, can help conserve memory by allowing shared libraries to be used by multiple applications simultaneously. In environments where many small applications are running, dynamically linked libraries save memory since they only need to be loaded once, regardless of how many applications utilize them. Employing lazy loading techniques—where dynamic libraries are only loaded into memory when called—can further optimize resource usage by minimizing the initial memory footprint.

Seamless resource management can also be achieved through the adoption of modular programming practices. By compartmentalizing code into smaller, functional modules, developers can link only those components required for specific tasks. This modular approach enables efficient resource allocation and usage, reducing the overall memory footprint. Additionally, it allows for easier maintenance, as individual modules can be updated or replaced without affecting the entire application.

Another critical technique for optimizing resource usage involves utilizing tools for profiling and analyzing performance. By employing profiling tools such as gprof or perf, developers can identify bottlenecks in their applications, which libraries are consuming the most resources, and areas where excessive memory allocation is occurring. Armed with this information, developers can make more informed decisions about optimizing linking strategies, identifying less efficient libraries, and implementing changes that enhance the overall efficiency of their applications.

Moreover, compression of resources can significantly reduce footprint and load times. Utilizing tools to compress binaries (e.g., UPX) and pack libraries into minimal distributions can help manage limited storage resources. However, this requires careful consideration as decompressing resources can increase CPU utilization, potentially counteracting space benefits. A balanced approach is critical in determining when compression is beneficial, especially in scenarios where computation speed is essential.

Implementing memory management practices such as pooling or using object allocation libraries can also contribute to resource optimization. By carefully managing dynamic memory allocation and lifecycle within the application, excessive fragmentations can be avoided. Allocating memory in blocks or using custom allocators designed specifically for embedded contexts can mitigate memory fragmentation issues common in constrained systems.

In scenarios involving embedded systems, it's crucial to adopt real-time optimization strategies to ensure efficient execution under workload demands. Real-time systems often need guaranteed response times; therefore, linking related functionalities into tightly-bound libraries could lead to faster execution, as linked components can access resources with minimal delay.

Finally, establishing a thorough testing and validation process is integral to ensuring that optimization efforts are successful. Implementing both unit tests and system tests helps confirm that applications function as expected after optimizations. This process should include tests for resource consumption, ensuring that the application performs within the constraints established.

In conclusion, optimizing for limited resources in the Linux ecosystem requires a multifaceted approach that fosters efficiency while ensuring application reliability. By carefully considering the constraints imposed by available hardware, utilizing static and dynamic linking strategies judiciously, adopting modular programming practices, profiling performance, employing memory management strategies, and validating with rigorous testing, developers can build lightweight applications that maintain a high level of performance in resource-constrained environments. These techniques collectively empower developers to navigate the challenges of optimization, resulting in robust, efficient software solutions that thrive under limitations.

12.3. Real-time Operations and Linking

Real-time operations in software development represent a critical area of focus, particularly when it comes to linking applications designed to function predictably within strict timing constraints. In Linux environments, real-time systems often require careful consideration of how libraries are linked to ensure that software can deliver the responsiveness and reliability needed for real-time operations.

In real-time systems, deterministic behavior is paramount. This means that the application must complete processing tasks within predefined time limits, making it essential to optimize every aspect of the software's execution. Linking plays a significant role in this by affecting how quickly functions from libraries are available to be called and executed. The speed of linking, whether static or dynamic, can impact the overall performance and responsiveness of real-time applications.

For real-time software, using static linking can be advantageous, as it compiles all necessary library code directly into the executable at compile time. This eliminates the dependency on external dynamic libraries during runtime that could introduce variability and latency. Statically linking libraries allows the entire application to load into memory at startup, which can yield faster execution times because the application does not have to search for and resolve symbols at runtime. This predictability is essential for systems that require guarantees on performance.

Conversely, dynamic linking offers its own set of advantages, particularly in terms of flexibility and memory usage. For applications that are less stringent regarding execution timing, dynamic linking can allow for the sharing of libraries among multiple processes. In real-time systems where many applications may run concurrently, this shared resource model can conserve memory, which is an important consideration for systems with limited resources. However, developers must carefully manage the loading times and dependencies of these libraries to avoid unpredictable delays that could violate timing constraints.

Another critical aspect is the handling of library updates. In real-time systems, stability is crucial, and any update to linked libraries can potentially disrupt the operation of the application. Therefore, methodologies for testing and validating library updates are essential. Automated regression tests can confirm that the application continues to behave predictably after a library update. Moreover, organizations may choose to implement version pinning for critical libraries to ensure that their applications always utilize the tested and verified versions, thus maintaining reliability.

Scheduling is another aspect of real-time operations that is influenced by linking practices. In systems designed to support multiple real-time tasks, the linker must ensure that the linkage of libraries does not introduce additional overhead that could disrupt the scheduling of tasks. This requires careful consideration of how resources are allocated within the shared libraries being used, as functions that may be called frequently should be optimized to access memory efficiently.

Additionally, developers must be vigilant about the performance implications of the linking choices they make. Profiling tools such as `gprof`, `perf`, and real-time tracing tools can provide insights into how linked functions contribute to overall system performance. Understanding function call frequencies and execution times helps identify critical paths within the application that need optimization, and where the impact of linking can be minimized to achieve better real-time performance.

Moreover, it is essential to keep in mind the security implications of linked libraries within real-time systems. A vulnerability in a dynamically linked library could pose a severe risk to the entire application, disrupting execution and potentially compromising the integrity of the system. Therefore, maintaining a proactive approach to library management, including regular security audits and using only trusted sources for library dependencies, is critical in preserving the robustness of real-time applications.

In summary, linking for real-time operations in Linux involves carefully balancing the need for performance, stability, and responsiveness. Static versus dynamic linking strategies must be specifically tailored to meet the timing requirements of the application while managing resource constraints effectively. Robust testing, library management procedures, and security assessments all contribute to ensuring that real-time systems can operate reliably under the unpredictable conditions they face. Emphasizing these principles equips developers with the insights they need to navigate the nuances of linking in real-time environments, ultimately leading to successful application outcomes.

12.4. Case Study: Linking for IoT

In this case study, we will delve into the unique challenges and strategies of linking in the context of Internet of Things (IoT) devices, an area that has gained significant attention amidst the rapid proliferation of connected devices that require robust and efficient linking techniques. IoT devices, characterized by their low power consumption, limited processing capabilities, and diverse operational environments, impose specific constraints on linking practices, which are essential for supporting the seamless functioning of these interconnected applications.

To start, it is essential to recognize that IoT devices often operate in a resource-constrained environment. This includes limitations in memory, processing power, and battery life. The linking of libraries for IoT applications must therefore prioritize lightweight and efficient libraries that cater to these constraints. Developers must thoughtfully evaluate which libraries provide the required functionalities without incurring excessive overhead. The choice of linking methods—static versus dynamic—becomes critical in this context. While static linking may enhance performance and reduce the risk of runtime errors by embedding library code directly into the executable, it can lead to larger binary sizes that may not be suitable for devices with limited flash memory. Conversely, dynamic linking offers flexibility in managing memory usage but could complicate runtime execution in environments where resources are tightly controlled.

A prominent aspect of linking in IoT devices is the need for real-time performance. Many IoT applications necessitate timely responses to events, whether monitoring sensor data or executing commands based on user inputs. This responsiveness depends significantly on how libraries are linked and how the application manages its dependencies. Real-time operating systems (RTOS) are often employed in IoT contexts, offering precise timing guarantees. To ensure compliance with these timing requirements, developers typically gravitate towards static linking, which avoids the unpredictability associated with the dynamic resolution of symbols at runtime.

Security also plays a pivotal role in the linking of IoT applications. IoT devices are often deployed in remote or unsecured locations, making them prime targets for cyberattacks. Consequently, developers must implement stringent security practices throughout the linking process. This includes avoiding the use of libraries that may have known vulnerabilities and ensuring that all external libraries adhere to security best practices. Furthermore, incorporating robust testing strategies and rigorous code reviews before linking third-party libraries can help prevent potential breaches that could expose the device or its data.

Another consideration for linking in IoT is the necessity for connectivity and interoperability. Many IoT devices operate within ecosystems, communicating with other devices and platforms. As such, developers must ensure that the libraries they employ facilitate seamless data exchange and conform to industry standards and protocols. This could involve linking with libraries designed for specific communication protocols such as MQTT, CoAP, or HTTP, which are essential for enabling communication between devices and cloud services. Here, it's essential to select libraries that are lightweight and optimized for low-bandwidth environments, where efficient data transmission is crucial.

Moreover, the rise of edge computing is shaping the landscape of IoT device linking by emphasizing the processing of data closer to the source, thereby reducing latency and bandwidth usage. As edge devices become more prevalent, linking strategies must adapt to incorporate components that allow for distributed processing. This translates into a modular approach to linking, where devices leverage libraries designed for edge computing capabilities, performing initial processing locally and dynamically linking to additional resources or cloud services as necessary for data analysis.

Finally, the developer community and ongoing support will be vital for successful linking practices in IoT applications. The open-source community has made significant contributions to the development of libraries and frameworks specifically tailored for IoT devices. Engaging with these communities can provide developers with access to best practices, troubleshooting support, and valuable resources for optimizing linking strategies. This collaborative spirit is essential for advancing the state of IoT technology and ensuring that best practices for linking and resource management evolve alongside this rapidly changing domain.

In summary, linking for IoT applications presents unique challenges stemming from resource constraints, real-time performance requirements, security considerations, interoperability needs, and the advent of edge computing. Balancing these aspects is essential for developers working within the IoT ecosystem, guiding their choices in library selection, linking strategies, and overall application design. By mastering these challenges and leveraging the vast resources available through community engagement, developers can create efficient and robust IoT solutions that meet the demands of the modern connected landscape.

13. Linking in Distributed Systems

13.1. Challenges in Distributed Environments

In the rapidly evolving landscape of distributed environments, linking applications presents unique challenges that require careful consideration and innovative strategies. Distributed systems, characterized by multiple interconnected components operating across different machines or locations, necessitate a linking approach that addresses the complexities of network communications, data sharing, and fault tolerance. As organizations increasingly turn to distributed architectures to enhance scalability, reliability, and performance, understanding these challenges becomes paramount for developers and systems architects.

One of the primary challenges in linking within distributed environments is managing communication between components that may reside on different machines. Unlike traditional applications where all components are hosted locally, distributed applications must coordinate data transfers across network boundaries. This adds latency, potential data bottlenecks, and the need for effective serialization and deserialization of data for smooth communication. When linking libraries that facilitate such communications—such as those handling remote procedure calls (RPC) or message queues—developers must ensure that the linked libraries are optimized for network efficiency, as any inefficiencies can degrade overall application performance.

Furthermore, interoperability becomes a critical issue in distributed systems. Different components may be developed using various programming languages, frameworks, or versions of libraries, leading to incompatibilities when attempting to link them together. Developers need to adopt a strategy that accounts for these variations, possibly leveraging interoperability libraries or interfaces such as gRPC, Apache Thrift, or RESTful APIs to facilitate smoother interactions. Establishing a unified API or data format for communication can mitigate these issues, improving integration and reducing friction.

Data consistency and state management is another crucial challenge in distributed systems linking. In environments where multiple processes or nodes are updating shared data, maintaining data consistency while linking different components can prove complex. Strategies like event-driven architectures, distributed transactions, or eventual consistency models may need to be integrated to ensure that all components remain synchronized. Libraries that help manage these states, such as those providing distributed caching or coordination services, must be linked while considering how they will maintain consistency across the system.

Fault tolerance is essential for distributed applications, as the likelihood of partial failures increases with the complexity of interconnected components. Robust link management involves ensuring that applications can handle failures gracefully, either by using retry mechanisms for linking operations, implementing circuit breakers, or switching to backup components when primary resources fail. When linking failover libraries or services, developers must carefully craft their linking strategies to ensure minimal disruption and maintain overall application functionality.

Security considerations also loom large within distributed systems. The act of linking libraries can expose vulnerabilities, especially when communication channels traverse external networks. Protecting data in transit through encryption, validating inputs, and ensuring that linked libraries are up to date with security patches become critical practices in a distributed environment. Techniques for managing secure links across distributed components need to be established, potentially incorporating frameworks focused on authentication and access control, such as OAuth or OpenID Connect, into the linked libraries.

Moreover, monitoring and observability play an essential role in managing linked applications within distributed systems. Extensive logging, metrics collection, and tracing should be integrated to track the interactions between linked components and diagnose issues swiftly. Linking observability libraries that provide this functionality opens pathways to enhance application performance, security, and reliability in distributed settings.

In summary, linking in distributed environments presents distinct challenges influenced by communication management, interoperability, data consistency, fault tolerance, and security concerns. By understanding and addressing these challenges, developers can adopt innovative linking strategies that enhance the performance and integrity of distributed applications. Emphasizing best practices and leveraging robust libraries designed for distributed operations will pave the way for effective linking solutions in increasingly complex distributed systems.

13.2. Cloud Computing Implications

In an increasingly interconnected world, the implications of cloud computing on linking practices in Linux environments are profound and multifaceted. Cloud computing introduces a new set of challenges and opportunities that affect how developers manage libraries and dependencies, which, in turn, shapes the performance, reliability, and scalability of applications. As applications transition to cloud-based architectures, understanding these implications is crucial for developers seeking to unlock the full potential of their software solutions.

One of the most significant implications of cloud computing on linking is the need for seamless library management and dependency resolution across distributed environments. Unlike traditional computing, where applications are typically deployed on a single physical machine, cloud architectures often involve multiple services hosted on different instances. In this context, developers must ensure that all components are accessing compatible library versions, which requires advanced dependency management strategies. Package managers integrated within cloud platforms can help automate these processes, allowing applications to dynamically link to the necessary libraries without manual intervention.

Additionally, the distributed nature of cloud environments raises questions about data locality and access speeds. Linking practices may need to adjust to prioritize libraries that optimize data access and minimize latency for cloud-hosted applications. For instance, libraries optimized for cloud interactions (such as those that handle RESTful APIs or data transfers to and from cloud databases) may need to be linked differently than traditional libraries. This can involve evaluating the performance and overhead associated with each library's functions to ensure that they provide optimal outcomes within a cloud context.

Moreover, cloud computing enables the use of microservices architectures, necessitating a modular approach to linking. In this context, individual microservices often rely on distinct libraries, each with its own dependencies. Developers must adopt a linking pattern that retains modularity while effectively managing inter-service communication. Containerization emerges as a pivotal practice that not only encapsulates libraries with services but also promotes the use of linking strategies that are lightweight and efficient. Technologies such as Docker facilitate the deployment of microservices with all dependencies included, ensuring that each service has access to the libraries it needs without dependency conflicts.

Another vital implication of cloud computing on linking involves the considerations of scalability. Applications deployed in cloud environments often need to scale horizontally, meaning that multiple instances of an application may run concurrently. Efficient linking practices must accommodate this scaling, ensuring that multiple instances can share libraries without consuming excessive resources. This can also involve ensuring that dynamically linked libraries are optimized for cloud redundancy and fault tolerance, allowing instances to rely on a shared library without introducing single points of failure.

Security implications are critical within cloud computing as well. When linking libraries in cloud environments, developers must adopt rigorous security practices to safeguard applications from external threats. This includes ensuring that only trusted libraries are linked, applying consistent security policies across instances, and validating that dependencies are up-to-date and free from vulnerabilities. The introduction of security tools designed for cloud environments can further enhance this process, allowing automated security checks to be integrated into the linking process.

Performance and cost management are another significant aspect connected to linking in cloud-based environments. Cloud providers typically charge based on resource consumption, which can include CPU cycles, memory usage, and data transfer. Developers must develop linking strategies that optimize these resources, reducing costs while ensuring sufficient performance for end users. Strategies such as incorporating caching mechanisms and prioritizing efficient library usage can lead to better resource allocation and cost-effective operation.

In summary, the implications of cloud computing on linking practices in Linux environments are vast and require a comprehensive under-standing of contemporary development challenges. By focusing on efficient dependency management, optimizing for cloud scalability, incorporating robust security practices, and considering cost and performance implications, developers can harness the opportunities presented by cloud computing to create resilient, efficient, and high-performing applications. Embracing these considerations entices developers to innovate continuously, shaping the future of linking in an ever-evolving software landscape.

13.3. Fault Tolerance in Linked Applications

In the growing landscape of distributed applications, ensuring fault tolerance in linked applications is paramount. Fault tolerance refers to the ability of a system to continue functioning correctly in the event of failures or errors. This involves incorporating robust error handling and recovery mechanisms into the application's architecture, partic-ularly during the linking phase where multiple components and libraries interact. For linked applications within distributed environ-ments, creating resilient systems that can gracefully handle faults is essential for maintaining reliability and availability.

One key strategy for enhancing fault tolerance in linked applications is to enhance library management. In distributed systems, applications often depend on numerous libraries, each potentially interacting with different components across a network. Developers must ensure that the libraries used are well-tested, reliable, and capable of handling errors proactively. This includes selecting libraries that have built-in error handling mechanisms, allowing them to manage exceptions and unexpected situations internally before propagating errors back to the application. Libraries should be regularly updated to address any known vulnerabilities, ensuring that potential points of failure are minimized.

Moreover, implementing redundancy within linked applications can significantly contribute to fault tolerance. By linking to multiple instances of critical libraries where appropriate—either through load balancing or failover strategies—applications can continue functioning in the event one instance fails. This redundancy can be achieved through various means, including clustering services and employing load balancers that can route requests to healthy instances of linked libraries or services. By managing link redundancy effectively, developers can create systems that maintain functionality even under adverse conditions.

Error detection mechanisms play a vital role in ensuring fault tolerance in linked applications. Developers should implement comprehensive logging and monitoring at various layers, from the application itself down to the libraries. These mechanisms provide insights into operational states, making it easier to detect anomalies or failures early. For example, linking libraries that provide detailed logging capabilities can offer valuable context during failures, simplifying diagnostics and troubleshooting efforts. When combined with alerting systems, such as monitoring dashboards or automated notifications, developers can respond swiftly to issues as they arise, ensuring that users experience minimal disruption.

Another aspect of fault tolerance that must be considered is graceful degradation. In environments where a linked library may experience an error or become unavailable, applications should be designed to degrade their functionalities rather than fail entirely. This could involve falling back to alternative libraries, reducing features, or providing informative error messages to users instead of simply crashing. By linking to lightweight libraries that support these fallback mechanisms, developers can enhance user experience even during adverse conditions.

Incorporating automated testing practices is also crucial to achieving fault tolerance in linked applications. Developing comprehensive test suites that validate the behavior of dependencies and their interactions can help catch issues early in the development lifecycle. Unit tests should focus on individual library functionalities, while integration tests should validate the interactions between multiple components. Ensuring that regression testing is included whenever an updated library is integrated will help reinforce the overall stability of the linked application, as any new faults introduced by library changes can be quickly identified and rectified.

For distributed systems, employing circuit breaker patterns can enhance fault tolerance significantly. When interacting with linked libraries or services, if a particular service call fails repeatedly, the circuit breaker can temporarily block access to the faulty component and allow for recovery. This prevents the entire application from becoming unresponsive due to one failing library or service, giving developers a chance to implement recovery strategies. By linking to resilient libraries that support this pattern, developers can create more reliable and fault-tolerant systems.

In summary, ensuring fault tolerance in linked applications is essential for the reliability of distributed systems. Through effective library management, redundancy, error detection, graceful degradation strategies, automated testing, and the implementation of circuit breaker patterns, developers can create applications that maintain robustness and availability even when faced with failures. Building systems with these strategies in mind will empower organizations to deliver consistently high-quality services, enhance user experience, and reduce downtime in an increasingly complex digital landscape. By prioritizing fault tolerance when developing linked applications, developers contribute to the overall resilience of the software systems on which users depend.

13.4. Network Topologies and System Linking

In the context of linking within distributed systems, network topologies play a pivotal role in determining how components communicate with one another and how libraries are linked across different nodes. The architecture of the network not only influences latency and bandwidth usage but also shapes the design of the application in terms of its library dependencies and the strategies for linking them effectively. As more applications emerge in distributed environments, understanding the relationship between network topologies and linking practices becomes essential for developing robust and performant systems.

One of the foundational elements to consider is the type of network topology in use. Common topologies in distributed systems include star, ring, mesh, and tree configurations, each with distinct implications for communication patterns and data flow. For instance, in a star topology, all nodes communicate through a central hub, which can lead to bottlenecks if the hub becomes overloaded or fails. This centralized nature may necessitate linking libraries that facilitate efficient data handling and coordination, as well as implementing redundancy through failover mechanisms to ensure system reliability.

Mesh topologies, on the other hand, offer a more resilient structure, where each node can directly communicate with multiple other nodes. This decentralized nature enables smaller, localized libraries to be linked more effectively, as libraries may be specifically tailored to handle interactions between adjacent nodes. This flexibility can lead to enhanced performance and fault tolerance, as messages can route around failures without reliance on a single point. Consequently, developers should consider how the mesh topology influences the linking of libraries in order to optimize communication and minimize delays.

When addressing linking strategies in cloud environments or service-oriented architectures, the principle of loose coupling becomes paramount. In such scenarios, libraries are linked in a way that promotes independence between components. This separation not only enables libraries to be updated or replaced without impacting other components but also allows for more flexible communication protocols, such as RESTful APIs or gRPC. By ensuring that each library can interact with its peers without being tightly bound to their implementations, developers can better design systems to operate efficiently within distributed topologies.

Additionally, the implications of bandwidth become a critical aspect in the context of network topologies and linking. In environments where bandwidth is limited, minimizing the volume of data exchanged between libraries and services is essential. Developers can leverage techniques such as data serialization to streamline data transfer, thereby reducing the overhead introduced by excessive library calls. Linked libraries that offer efficient serialization mechanisms should be prioritized, as these can help conserve bandwidth while maintaining high performance during data exchanges.

Security considerations also come into play when examining the influence of network topologies on linking. In distributed systems with numerous connected devices, ensuring that libraries are correctly linked and securely communicate with one another is crucial. When libraries are linked in environments where data is transmitted over open networks, implementing encryption and secure communication protocols becomes imperative. This might involve linking security libraries that ensure data exchanged between nodes is protected against interception or tampering, safeguarding application integrity in distributed topologies.

Finally, fault tolerance strategies are intrinsically tied to network topologies and linking practices. Developers must consider how failures—whether in libraries or network components—are handled during the linking process. For instance, employing circuit breaker patterns or fallback libraries can help ensure that libraries remain functional even in the face of unexpected errors. Understanding the implications of network failures and how these relate to linked libraries helps build resilience into applications operating in distributed environments.

In conclusion, network topologies significantly influence the linking practices used in distributed systems. The choice of network design dictates how libraries interact, informs the strategies for reducing latency and bandwidth usage, influences security considerations, and shapes the overall architecture of the application. Developers must thoughtfully evaluate these traits when designing linked applications within distributed environments to ensure they meet performance expectations while maintaining reliability and robustness in the face of varying conditions. Effective linking practices in the context of network topologies can elevate the overall quality and functionality of distributed systems.

14. Virtualization and Links

14.1. Understanding Virtualization Basics

In exploring the intricacies of linking within the context of virtualization and linked libraries, it is essential to first understand how virtualization has transformed modern software development and deployment. Virtualization allows organizations to create isolated environments within a single physical hardware setup, whether through virtual machines (VMs) or lightweight containers. This flexibility provides developers with the ability to efficiently manage resources, rapidly deploy applications, and create environments tailored to their specific needs.

However, this innovation brings with it a host of unique challenges —particularly concerning how libraries are shared, linked, and optimized in these virtualized environments. As developers begin to build applications that are cloud-native and designed for container deployment, understanding these challenges becomes crucial.

In a virtualized environment, library sharing can occur at various levels. For instance, container technologies like Docker provide a mechanism to bundle an application along with its dependencies into a single container image. This approach allows multiple applications to share common libraries while minimizing overhead. However, when linking libraries in containers, developers must consciously make choices about which libraries should be linked statically versus dynamically, weighing the trade-offs between space efficiency and the need for flexibility in updates.

Within VMs, the situation can be more complex, given that each VM functions as an isolated environment with its own operating system instance. This isolation means that library linking must be handled at the VM level without impacting other VMs running on the same host. The management of shared libraries across VMs may require careful configuration to ensure that each VM can access necessary libraries while avoiding version conflicts. Here, developers can leverage shared storage solutions or package management systems that facilitate cross-VM access to common libraries, enabling efficient updates across multiple instances.

For optimization within virtual spaces, various strategies can be employed. One notable method is the use of image layering in containers. When managing the linking of libraries in Docker, utilizing a multi-stage build process can help to optimize the final image size by separating the build environment from the production environment. By carefully managing the layers in this manner, developers can reduce the overall resource footprint while ensuring that only necessary libraries and dependencies are linked into the final image.

Evaluating performance in virtualized environments also requires developers to be mindful of I/O operations and network latency that can be introduced by virtualization overhead. Testing libraries for performance within virtual environments ensures that interactions with linked libraries remain efficient and that applications do not incur unnecessary delays in execution. Profiling tools can help identify performance bottlenecks and provide insights into how libraries are interacting under virtualized conditions.

The case studies of linking in containerized applications, particularly in the context of microservices, reveal both the advantages and challenges of managing linked libraries. In microservices, different services may rely on different versions of the same libraries, necessitating effective version management and compatibility assessments. Utilizing tools like service mesh can help direct traffic between services, manage API calls, and provide increased visibility into how libraries are being used across the microservice landscape.

Moreover, when organizations deploy applications in public cloud environments, understanding how orchestration tools like Kubernetes manage linked containers is vital. Kubernetes automates the deployment, scaling, and operation of application containers, while also managing the associated libraries. Here, resource allocation and redundancy become central to ensuring that services are reliably linked and that libraries maintain their integrity and performance.

As developers delve deeper into virtualization under various constraints, they must also consider the relationship between virtualization and security. Proper security measures, such as ensuring that only trusted libraries are linked within containers or VMs, become critical to mitigating risks associated with vulnerabilities in linked components. Continuous monitoring and vulnerability scanning tools can protect the integrity of linked libraries throughout the development and deployment cycles.

In conclusion, the challenges presented by virtualization in linked applications require developers to be strategic and informed in their approach. From managing library sharing in containers to optimizing linking practices in VMs, navigating these complexities is essential for creating robust, high-performance applications. Understanding these relationships and continually adapting to evolving practices will enable developers to fully harness the benefits of virtualization while mitigating the associated risks. Embracing these challenges will pave the way for innovative linking practices across an ever-expanding landscape of virtualized systems.

14.2. Virtual Environments and Library Sharing

In the digital age, libraries and linking practices are not merely technical processes; they encapsulate essential methodologies that significantly shape the functionality and performance of applications within virtual environments. The advent of virtualization technologies has transformed how libraries are handled, ultimately affecting software deployment and resource utilization. In this comprehensive examination of 'Virtual Environments and Library Sharing,' we dive deeply into the mechanisms by which virtual machines (VMs) and containers manage libraries, and explore the implications of these practices on development cycles and application performance.

Virtualization allows for the creation of multiple isolated instances of an operating system on a single physical server—each instance referred to as a virtual machine. At the same time, containerization enables developers to package applications and their dependencies into lightweight containers that run on any compatible system. Both approaches facilitate efficient resource management, scalability, and isolation, but they handle libraries, linking, and sharing differently.

In a VM-based environment, each instance runs a complete operating system and has its own filesystem, which includes its own libraries. This isolation presents a challenge when it comes to resource efficiency, as multiple VMs might end up maintaining redundant copies of the same libraries, consuming larger amounts of storage and memory. While VMs can offer flexibility in library sharing through shared volumes or mounted storage, the performance overhead associated with managing these shared resources can hinder operational efficiency.

Conversely, the container paradigm optimizes library sharing by allowing applications to leverage shared libraries that reside in a single layered filesystem. When a container is created, it builds upon a base image that can include common libraries. This characteristic drastically lowers redundancy since multiple containers can utilize the same library versions without duplicating them. However, this shared approach necessitates careful attention to library version management to ensure compatibility and prevent conflicts, particularly in microservice architectures where many services rely on different versions of libraries.

One significant efficiency gained from linking in containers is a reduced footprint. While traditional applications may consist of bundled executables with their entire library dependencies, containers can allow an application to remain agile and compact by dynamically linking to common libraries at runtime. This strategy not only accelerates deployment but can also minimize memory usage, which is crucial for environments where resources are constrained. That said, it also places the impetus on developers to ensure that the underlying libraries are consistently available and configured correctly in the container images.

Linking practices in virtual environments also embrace dynamic loading, which enables applications to load libraries on-demand rather than at startup. This optimization allows applications to remain responsive, particularly in environments exposed to variable workloads, since libraries are only loaded when their functionalities are required. The dynamic linking strategy aligns well with the principles of resource conservation, ensuring that only necessary components are active at any given time.

However, as applications increasingly rely on libraries hosted externally or within microservices, network dependency and its associated latency become primary considerations. Applications in virtualized or containerized environments must maintain a balance between the flexibility of linking with external libraries and the overhead of potential communication delays. To address this, developers often adopt strategies that enhance network communication, such as using optimized messaging protocols or data serialization methods that minimize the payload size transmitted between services.

Security is another critical consideration when linking libraries in virtualized environments. The shared nature of containers means that a vulnerability within one library can potentially compromise every container relying on it. Developers must therefore adopt meticulous library management practices, employing tools to scan for known vulnerabilities and ensuring that libraries are up-to-date. Moreover, incorporating practices like immutable images—where container images are not modified after they are built—can help enhance security as only trusted libraries are relegated to the image, reducing exposure to vulnerabilities.

As more organizations adopt cloud-native development practices, the role of the developer community becomes increasingly pivotal. Open-source libraries now provide a wealth of resources for developers working in virtual and containerized environments. Engaging with the community provides insights into optimal practices, and awareness of the challenges faced by others can inspire collaborative solutions.

In conclusion, the ways in which virtual machines and containers handle libraries and linking represents a significant evolution in software development practices within the Linux ecosystem. By effectively navigating the paradigm of virtualization and prioritizing efficient library management, developers can harness the advantages of both virtualization and containerization, ultimately leading to performant, scalable, and resilient applications. As technology continues to evolve, the integration of continuous learning and community engagement plays a crucial role in adapting linking practices, ensuring that developers are equipped to meet the demands of modern software development within virtual environments.

14.3. Optimization within Virtual Spaces

Optimization within Virtual Spaces is a crucial aspect of building high-performance, resource-efficient applications in the rapidly evolving landscape of software development, particularly when dealing with virtualization and containerization technologies. Virtual environments, including virtual machines (VMs) and containers, offer flexibility and scalability but also introduce unique challenges regarding how libraries are linked and how dependencies are managed.

First and foremost, developers must consider how to optimize library usage in these virtualized environments. One approach is to use shared libraries effectively, allowing multiple applications to link against a single instance of a library rather than bundling redundant copies into each application. This sharing reduces disk space usage and memory consumption, leading to a more efficient deployment in environments with limited resources. In containerized applications, developers should prioritize linking to lightweight libraries that encapsulate essential features without unnecessary overhead, avoiding the bloat that can stem from heavy-weight frameworks.

Furthermore, understanding the implications of image layering in containerization is imperative for optimization. Containers often build upon base images that can include core libraries. By employing a multi-stage build process, developers can separate the build environment from the final production environment, ensuring that only the necessary libraries are included in the final image. This process not only reduces the overall size of the container but also enhances security, as unnecessary development tools and libraries are eliminated.

To further enhance efficiency, developers should embrace lazy loading techniques when linking libraries in virtualized environments. Instead of loading all libraries at startup, applications can defer the loading of specific libraries until their functionalities are required. This strategy conserves memory and accelerates application startup times, providing a smoother user experience, particularly in environments with strict resource constraints.

Profile-guided optimizations can also play a transformative role in achieving efficiency in virtual spaces. By using profiling tools to analyze application performance, developers can identify which linked libraries and functions are consuming the most resources. Insights gained from analyzing execution paths allow for more informed decisions on optimizing links, whether that involves inlining critical functions, eliminating unnecessary dependencies, or refining data structures utilized in linked libraries to enhance performance.

Additionally, conducting thorough load testing in virtualized environments is essential for assessing the impact of specific linking strategies on application performance. Load testing can help identify bottlenecks and assess how applications respond under varying loads and configurations. By simulating real-world usage patterns, developers can gather valuable metrics related to resource consumption, response time, and throughput, enabling them to optimize linking practices accordingly.

Another crucial aspect of optimization within virtual spaces is addressing the security implications of linking libraries. In virtualized environments, shared libraries can pose risks if they are not properly vetted or maintained. Continuous monitoring of linked libraries through automated scanners can identify vulnerabilities, ensuring timely updates and mitigating risks. Security best practices like using minimal base images for containers and adhering to the principle of least privilege when granting access to libraries contribute to a more secure linking process.

Finally, enhancing collaboration through community engagement can drive further optimization. Open-source projects often maintain repositories of optimized libraries tailored for specific use cases, allowing developers to benefit from community-driven innovations. By contributing back to these projects, sharing performance insights, and collaborating on improvements, developers can significantly impact future optimization practices.

In conclusion, optimization within virtual spaces involves a multifaceted approach that encompasses efficient library usage, employing lazy loading techniques, leveraging profiling insights, conducting thorough load testing, maintaining robust security practices, and encouraging community collaboration. By adopting these optimization strategies, developers can create high-performance applications capable of thriving in the complex virtualized environments that dominate modern computing landscapes. Such practices not only enhance application performance but also contribute to efficient resource utilization and sustainable software development practices.

14.4. Case Studies in Containerized Linking

In the subchapter 'Case Studies in Containerized Linking', we delve into practical examples and insights derived from the real-world application of linking practices within containerized environments. With the advent of container technologies such as Docker and Kubernetes, new paradigms for managing dependencies and linking libraries have emerged. These case studies illustrate the innovative strategies developers employ to optimize linking processes, tackle challenges, and leverage the unique advantages of containerized architectures.

The first case study focuses on a multi-tiered web application deployed in a cloud environment. This application consists of various microservices, each responsible for specific functionalities such as user authentication, data processing, and payment handling. By utilizing a microservices architecture, each service can independently scale, deploy, and link with relevant libraries.

In this scenario, the developers opted for dynamic linking to share common libraries across microservices, such as logging and data manipulation libraries. This decision significantly reduced the footprint of individual container images without sacrificing functionality. However, the challenge arose when different services required varying versions of the same library. The team implemented a strategy where each microservice included a specific version of the dependent libraries in its Dockerfile, coupled with semantic versioning practices to manage compatibility effectively. This approach minimized dependency conflicts and facilitated consistent builds while allowing teams to work on services in parallel without hindrance.

Another case study examines an IoT application where a set of interconnected sensor devices gathers and processes environmental data. In this use case, the developers faced constraints due to the limited resources of the sensor hardware, necessitating careful selection and linking of lightweight libraries. The team chose static linking for critical libraries that were performance-sensitive to ensure that the essential functionalities could be accessed swiftly and predictably.

To optimize the size of the final binaries, the developers utilized multi-stage builds in their Docker setup. This approach involved compiling the application and libraries in an initial stage while only copying the necessary output into a final, minimal image. The outcome was a streamlined container that could be deployed efficiently across the range of IoT devices without redundancy.

In a different context, let's consider a distributed data processing application running in a cloud-native environment. The application consisted of microservices responsible for data extraction, transformation, and loading (ETL) processes. The developers required efficient library linkage to manage the myriad transformations applied to incoming data streams. To facilitate this, they used container orchestration to dynamically scale the number of instances based on interface load.

The application leveraged shared libraries for data transformations, allowing different microservices to access and utilize common functions without separately linked libraries. Through a central artifact repository, the team managed library versions, guaranteeing cohesive library usage across services. In practice, they deployed tools like Artifactory to help maintain the repository and facilitate seamless access to libraries, enhancing the overall linking and management process.

These case studies demonstrate that successful linking practices in containerized environments often stem from innovative strategies tailored to unique application requirements. By adopting patterns such as dynamic linking, implementing effective version control for dependencies, and prioritizing lightweight design, developers can navigate the complexities of linking applications in the cloud and IoT spaces effectively.

Going forward, there are opportunities for further exploration and adaptation of linking strategies as containerization technology continues to evolve. Emerging trends, such as serverless computing and edge computing, present new challenges but also offer enticing possibilities to optimize linking at the same time. Developers must stay abreast of these advancements, ensuring their linking practices remain efficient and agile within rapidly changing environments.

In conclusion, the case studies on containerized linking underscore the importance of flexibility, efficiency, and innovation in managing dependencies and integrating libraries. By leveraging modern containerization technology creatively, developers can build robust applications that seamlessly connect with the myriad components in today's software ecosystems. Understanding and applying these strategies will remain essential as organizations continue to adopt container-oriented development practices in the pursuit of delivering high-performing, resource-efficient applications.

15. Customizing Linkers for Specific Needs

15.1. Tailoring Linker Scripts

Tailoring linker scripts is a fundamental aspect of managing the linking process in software development, especially in the intricate landscape provided by the Linux operating system. Linker scripts empower developers to customize how object files and libraries are combined during the linking phase, allowing for optimization in terms of memory layout, execution speed, and application architecture. This section will delve into the methodologies, best practices, and practical applications for creating tailored linker scripts that meet specific developer needs.

At its core, a linker script serves as a text file that provides instructions to the linker on how to arrange and organize sections of code and data in the final executable. By manipulating these sections, developers can control the memory layout of their applications, which is particularly crucial in embedded systems or performance-critical applications where resource constraints dictate design decisions.

One of the first steps in creating a custom linker script is to define the memory regions that will be utilized within the application. This is typically done using the MEMORY command, which allows developers to specify address ranges, permissions, and memory types. For example:

```
MEMORY {
    FLASH (rx) : ORIGIN = 0x08000000, LENGTH = 128K
    RAM (rw) : ORIGIN = 0x20000000, LENGTH = 20K
}
```

In this snippet, the developer has defined two memory regions: FLASH memory for read-only storage of executable code and RAM for read-write operations. This foundational step allows for fine-grained control over where specific sections of the code will reside, which is critical for optimizing memory usage and performance.

Following the definition of memory regions, the next step involves detailing how different sections of the code should be organized. This

145

is where the SECTIONS command comes into play. By specifying how input sections from object files should be mapped to output sections in the executable, developers can optimize memory usage and ensure that critical functions are loaded efficiently. For instance:

```
SECTIONS {
    .text : {
        *(.text)
        *(.rodata)
    } > FLASH

    .data : {
        *(.data)
    } > RAM

    .bss : {
        *(.bss)
        *(COMMON)
    } > RAM
}
```

This custom linker script outlines where specific segments of the application's code will be located in memory. The .text and .rodata sections are placed in FLASH, while the .data and .bss segments are allocated in RAM. This control over memory layout can lead to significant optimizations, particularly in environments with constrained resources.

Beyond basic segment placements, linker scripts can include commands for various optimizations, such as alignment and address specification. Proper alignment of sections can improve access speed; therefore, using commands to specify alignment constraints can ensure that structures are memory-efficient and fast to access:

```
    .text ALIGN(4) : {
        *(.text)
    }
```

In addition to memory layout optimizations, custom linker scripts can be powerful tools for managing versioning and symbol visibility.

Developers can use specific configurations within their scripts to control which symbols are exported from shared libraries, impacting how libraries are linked and used across different applications. For example:

```
EXPORT_SYMBOLS {
    my_function;
}
```

Defining the export symbols can help ensure that only necessary symbols are exposed, which is crucial for encapsulation and maintaining proper dependencies in larger systems.

Template scripts can be employed as a base framework for many linking scenarios, enhancing productivity by providing common patterns that can be adapted for specific projects. By developing a library of standard practices and patterns, teams can streamline their linking processes, repeating successes without reinventing the wheel each time a project begins.

Moreover, continuous testing and validation of the custom linker scripts is essential to ensure correctness. Integrating these scripts into continuous integration (CI) pipelines allows developers to catch errors early in the process, ensuring that whenever updates are made to the code or structure of libraries, the linking remains efficient and accurate.

In summary, tailoring linker scripts is a powerful strategy for optimizing the linking process in applications running on Linux. By carefully defining memory layouts, organizing sections, controlling symbol visibility, and leveraging best practices, developers can maximize performance and efficiency. Through continuous refinement and integration with modern development practices such as CI/CD, the efficacy of custom linker scripts can significantly enhance application performance and resource management, paving the way for innovative software solutions that meet diverse needs.

15.2. Case Study: Custom Linkers in Use

In the realm of software development, the efficient and effective linking of libraries is crucial for optimizing application performance and ensuring seamless functionality. Custom linkers represent a powerful solution for developers seeking to tailor the linking process to their unique needs, accommodating specific requirements within their applications. The following case study illustrates how custom linkers can be effectively utilized to enhance linking practices, demonstrating real-world examples of successful implementations.

Custom Linker Use Cases

A prime example can be found in the aerospace industry, where software reliability is critical. A team of engineers responsible for developing an avionics system recognized that their traditional linking methods were introducing latency that could jeopardize performance when interfacing with safety-critical components. To address this issue, they developed a custom linker that employed advanced algorithms specifically designed to optimize symbol resolution and memory allocation, minimizing the delays associated with library loading and function linkage. This approach allowed them to achieve deterministic response times, crucial in real-time avionics applications.

In another instance, a developer-focused open-source application sought to support a wide range of plugins, each requiring different external libraries. Recognizing the complexities posed by conventional linking techniques, the development team opted to implement a custom linker capable of handling dynamic dependencies on-the-fly. This linker allowed the application to load and unload plugins along with their dependencies seamlessly while ensuring minimal memory overhead. By utilizing this custom linking architecture, the application maintained high-performance standards and improved user experience through quick and efficient plugin integration.

Evaluating Custom Solutions

When it comes to evaluating custom linker solutions, several metrics and criteria should be considered to ensure that the implementation meets the intended goals effectively. First and foremost, performance metrics such as linking speed, memory utilization, and runtime efficiency must be assessed. These metrics should be compared against baseline performance from prior linking methods to measure the actual improvements achieved through the custom linker.

Stability and reliability are also crucial factors to consider. An effective custom linker should demonstrate a high level of resilience to changes in libraries or application code without introducing breaking changes. Rigorous testing, including unit tests and regression tests, should be implemented to ensure the linker's functionality across various scenarios.

Scalability is another valuable metric, particularly in distributed or modular systems. A custom linker that can effectively manage an increasing number of dependencies or connect to multiple plugins must be able to exhibit consistent performance levels, irrespective of the application's size or complexity.

Lastly, maintainability and ease of integration into existing development workflows should also be taken into account. Developers should be able to adopt and adapt the custom linker with relative ease, ensuring that it can be integrated into continuous integration (CI) pipelines without causing significant disruption to established practices.

Managing Custom Solutions

Managing custom linking setups involves implementing best practices that safeguard performance while ensuring long-term reliability and maintainability. One key practice is documentation; developers should maintain thorough and up-to-date documentation regarding the custom linker, including its architecture, features, and usage patterns. Clear documentation will assist new team members in understanding how to effectively integrate and utilize the custom linker within their development workflows.

Version control is another essential practice—developing custom linkers often involves continuous iterations and updates. Using a version control system like Git to manage changes to the linker codebase provides a transparent way to track progress, facilitate collaboration among team members, and roll back changes if issues arise.

Regular benchmarking and profiling of the custom linker should be performed to assess its performance over time, especially in response to new libraries or application requirements. Performance fall-off can indicate potential inefficiencies that may have emerged, prompting timely optimizations.

Collaboration within the developer community is invaluable when managing custom linking solutions. Engaging with others in related fields can lead to insights into best practices and advancements in linker technology. Participating in open-source projects or contributing to community forums can broaden understanding and foster continuous learning.

In conclusion, the case study on customizing linkers demonstrates their potential in addressing unique needs in software linking practices. This exploration highlights successful implementations, evaluation strategies, and management best practices that developers can leverage—ultimately leading to enhanced performance, reliability, and maintainability in library linking processes across diverse applications. The future of linking conceivably hinges on the continued refinement and exploration of custom linker solutions, as developers strive to meet the demands of complex and resource-constrained environments.

15.3. Evaluating Custom Solutions

Evaluating custom solutions for linking practices in Linux requires a comprehensive analysis of a variety of metrics and considerations that can determine the effectiveness of a custom linker. As software development moves towards more complex systems, a tailored approach becomes essential in ensuring that linking processes are efficient, performant, and meet the specific needs of applications.

One of the key metrics for evaluating custom linking solutions is performance. Performance assessments should begin with measuring linking speed—how quickly the linker can resolve dependencies and produce usable binaries. This involves benchmarking the time taken to link various executable files and libraries to establish a performance baseline. Developers should compare these link times with conventional linking methods to quantify performance improvements brought about by custom solutions.

Another important aspect of performance evaluation involves examining memory usage. The custom linker should ideally minimize the final application footprint. This can be assessed by analyzing how much memory is allocated during the linking process and how much of that memory remains used after execution. Tools designed for analyzing memory usage, such as Valgrind or other profiling tools, will help developers visualize the allocated resources and identify possible inefficiencies resulting from the linking process.

In addition to performance and memory usage, stability and reliability metrics are paramount. A custom linker must maintain a low failure rate, particularly in production environments where stability is critical. Implementing rigorous testing methods and running regression tests on linked applications will provide insights into the consistency and reliability of the custom linking process. Monitoring and logging can provide valuable data to identify potential points of failure over time.

Given the dynamic nature of libraries and the potential for updates, another critical consideration is manageability and maintainability. Custom linkers should be designed to allow easy updates and maintenance without reworking extensive amounts of code. This means capturing and documenting the linking setup clearly, providing specifics on which libraries are linked, their configurations, and any dependencies involved. Version control systems, such as Git, are valuable for tracking changes in custom linkers, facilitating easy rollbacks and collaborative development.

Security considerations play a vital role in evaluating custom linking solutions as well. Developers should assess how the custom linker manages vulnerabilities related to linked libraries and the implications of linking untrusted or outdated libraries within applications. This includes evaluating existing security protocols and practices that are built into the linking process, ensuring compliance with best practices that minimize exposure to unauthorized access or exploitation of vulnerabilities.

User experience metrics can also be considered in evaluating custom solutions. For linked applications, it's important to measure user satisfaction—this can include tracking responsiveness and overall application performance from the user's perspective. Custom linkers that positively impact these metrics can significantly enhance the appeal of applications provided by developers.

Finally, community feedback and external validation can provide additional insights when evaluating custom linking solutions. Engaging with other developers and seeking their input through forums, workshops, or collaborative efforts can yield reflections on the practices employed and recommendations for improvements. Participating in open-source communities can also help validate the effectiveness of custom solutions against a broader set of use cases and experiences.

In summary, evaluating custom linker solutions requires a multifaceted approach that encompasses performance metrics, memory usage assessments, stability and reliability testing, maintainability considerations, security evaluations, user experience metrics, and community engagement. By carefully analyzing these aspects, developers can ensure that their custom linking solutions not only meet their specific needs but also contribute to robust and high-performing applications in the Linux ecosystem. Adopting these evaluative practices will guide developers in enhancing linking methodologies, fostering continuous improvement, and supporting successful outcomes across diverse software projects.

15.4. Managing Custom Solutions

Managing custom solutions for linking in software development is a vital aspect of ensuring efficiency, reliability, and performance, particularly in complex systems where libraries and dependencies play a crucial role. Custom linkers and tailored linking practices allow developers to address specific project requirements while optimizing the linking process. Below, we explore various strategies and best practices that aid in effectively managing custom linking solutions.

One primary strategy for managing custom solutions involves defining clear objectives and requirements for the linking process. Start by establishing what aspects of the linking process need optimization or customization in your project. This could involve performance metrics, memory usage, compatibility with specific libraries, or compliance with organizational standards. Having well-defined goals directs the focus of your custom linker development, ensuring it meets the project's unique needs effectively.

Next, meticulous documentation is essential throughout the development and maintenance of custom linkers. Detailed documentation that includes the architecture, configuration options, and usage instructions will help other developers or team members understand the linker's functionality and how to utilize it within their workflows. This is particularly important for onboarding new developers or refreshing the memory of existing team members regarding custom solutions. Additionally, documenting changes and updates to the linker will create a valuable historical record that will aid future enhancements and troubleshooting.

Integration of version control practices is another critical aspect of managing custom linking solutions. Utilizing systems like Git allows developers to track changes made to the linker and its associated configuration files. This capability enables the team to maintain a history of modifications, facilitating easier rollbacks when issues arise. Emphasizing branching strategies and pull requests can enable thorough reviews and discussions regarding modifications before they are merged into the main development branch, ultimately enhancing the quality and integrity of your linking solutions.

Continuous testing and validation play a fundamental role in managing custom linking setups. Regularly testing linked applications helps identify faults or regressions introduced through changes to the linker or libraries. Automate unit tests and regression tests to ensure that every update applied to the linker is validated against functional requirements. Running these tests within a continuous integration (CI) pipeline provides consistent feedback, enabling rapid identification of issues that could affect application performance.

Another critical area involves performance monitoring and assessment of linked applications. By profiling applications after linking, developers can gain insights into specific areas where linking practices may be causing bottlenecks. Embracing tools like gprof, Valgrind, or perf enables developers to analyze execution paths, measure function call frequencies, and pinpoint where optimizations are necessary. Incorporate this feedback loop to make iterative improvements in both linking strategies and the linker itself.

Managing custom solutions for linking requires not only an understanding of technical requirements but also proper change management protocols. When libraries or dependencies change, it's essential to assess the impact on the linking process and determine if adjustments are required in the custom linker. Establishing schedules for regular reviews of library dependencies and ensuring security updates are timely applied will help keep linked applications secure and optimized for performance.

Collaboration with the broader development community can significantly enhance the effectiveness of custom linking solutions. Engaging with forums, mailing lists, and communities focused on open-source development provides exposure to best practices, troubleshooting advice, and insights into prevalent standards in adjacent projects. By communicating with a network of developers and contributors, insights into effective strategies or potential pitfalls can emerge, guiding the evolution of your linking practices.

Another important aspect is the anticipation of future expansions. As applications grow in functionality or scale, custom solutions may require modifications to accommodate new features or integrations. Utilizing a modular design approach when developing a custom linker allows for flexibility in making enhancements without compromising existing functionality. During initial design, think about how to structure your linker for simplicity and scalability to manage anticipated future demands.

Finally, regularly revisiting and updating your linking practices to stay aligned with advancements in software development trends is crucial. New optimization techniques, coding paradigms, and technologies emerge at a rapid pace. By staying informed and open to adapting linking strategies, developers can ensure their custom solutions remain relevant and effective in the ever-evolving software landscape.

In conclusion, successfully managing custom linking solutions in software development demands a comprehensive approach that encompasses clear objectives, meticulous documentation, version control, continuous testing, performance monitoring, collaboration, and proactive planning for future needs. By embracing these best practices, developers can optimize their linking strategies, leading to more efficient and robust applications while harnessing the full power of the libraries at their disposal. These practices pave the way for meaningful improvements in software quality, maintainability, and responsiveness within complex systems.

16. Kernel-Level Linking

16.1. The Role of the Kernel in Linking

The kernel plays a crucial role in linking within the Linux operating system, influencing how libraries and application code interact. In Linux, the kernel is responsible for managing system resources, including memory, process scheduling, and device I/O. When it comes to linking, the kernel manages the loading of necessary libraries, resolving symbols, and ensuring that applications can access the required resources efficiently.

At the core of the linking process is the dynamic linker, known as ld.so (or ld-linux.so). This specialized component of the kernel takes charge upon program execution, loading dynamically linked libraries (shared objects) into memory. It uses a set of predefined rules to locate the libraries specified in an executable's header while maintaining a lookup cache to quickly resolve symbols during execution. This caching mechanism significantly speeds up the lookup and linking process, making applications more responsive.

The kernel also manages memory allocation for linked libraries, ensuring that multiple processes can share the same instance of a library without duplicating memory usage. This is especially important in environments with limited resources, such as embedded systems. When different processes require access to the same library, the kernel ensures that it remains loaded in memory, allowing for efficient execution and reducing overall system footprint.

Linking in the kernel involves not only the initial loading of libraries but also the management of library updates and versioning. When a shared library is updated, the kernel must ensure that all running processes can utilize the latest version without requiring them to be restarted. This dynamic ability to replace libraries while applications continue to function is one of the advantages of using shared libraries in linking.

Moreover, the kernel's handling of linking includes managing the visibility and accessibility of symbols between different libraries and applications. Every linked library exports certain symbols for use, while also maintaining the integrity of private symbols that should not be exposed to other components. The kernel facilitates this by ensuring that the correct version of a symbol is resolved based on the linking context of each application.

Despite the kernel's efficiency in managing linking, developers must remain vigilant regarding potential pitfalls associated with linked libraries, such as version mismatches or incompatibilities that can arise when a library is updated. The kernel provides mechanisms to handle these issues, including thorough error messages and diagnostics when linking errors occur.

Furthermore, as applications and libraries evolve, the Linux kernel interacts with tools and frameworks that promote best practices in linking. This may include leveraging package managers that automate library installations, ensuring that applications always link against the compatible versions of their dependencies.

In conclusion, the kernel serves as the backbone of linking in the Linux operating system, effectively managing library loading, memory allocation, symbol resolution, and version control. With its comprehensive oversight, the kernel ensures that linked applications function efficiently and reliably, enabling developers to harness the power of shared libraries without compromising performance or stability. Understanding the kernel's role in linking allows developers to create better applications that are optimized for the Linux environment.

16.2. Linking Directly within the Kernel

Linking Directly within the Kernel

Linking directly within the kernel presents an intriguing dimension of software development and systems engineering, particularly as we consider the intricate relationship between the operating system and the applications it supports. Using kernel-level linking as a mechanism to facilitate library management and resolve dependencies offers developers unique advantages and challenges, particularly concerning performance, security, and complexity. The kernel is not merely a facilitator of resource management; it plays a dynamic role in how libraries are linked, managed, and utilized by applications operating in tandem with the underlying system.

At the foundation of linking directly within the kernel is the concept of modules. The Linux kernel supports loadable kernel modules (LKMs) that allow developers to extend kernel functionality without recompiling the entire kernel. This dynamic linking method permits the addition of features and capabilities, such as hardware drivers, network protocols, or filesystem types, while keeping the kernel code lightweight and efficient.

Modules are linked into the kernel using the `insmod` (insert module) or `modprobe` command, which loads the specified module into the kernel's address space. This linkage is crucial, as the kernel acts as the orchestrator of system resources while managing how these modules interact with other kernel components. Unlike traditional linking, where the focus is primarily on executable files, kernel linking engenders a deeper integration that allows modules to directly access kernel functions, data structures, and resources, making it highly relevant for developers working on system-level applications.

The flexibility of kernel linking necessitates strong awareness of external dependencies and symbol visibility. Each module can export specific symbols that other modules can reference during execution. However, care must be taken to ensure that symbol conflicts—where two or more modules refer to the same symbol—are managed effectively to prevent errors or unpredictable behavior. Conversely, the kernel provides mechanisms such as symbol namespaces to avoid conflicts, helping maintain clean boundaries between modules operating in the same environment.

Efficiency is paramount when linking directly within the kernel. Kernel developers must prioritize performance to ensure that any additional functionality introduced via modules does not lead to degradation in system responsiveness. The linking process should be optimized to minimize overhead; this can involve strategies such as inline functions for frequently called kernel routines or utilizing preemptive mechanisms to ensure that time-sensitive operations are not disrupted by lengthy linkage overhead.

Security considerations loom large in the context of kernel linking. As the kernel serves as the critical interface between hardware and applications, any vulnerabilities in modules can lead to significant security risks. Developers should adopt robust practices to validate module integrity, including cryptographic signing and careful management of module permissions to prevent unauthorized access. Any libraries linked within the kernel context must be thoroughly vetted and kept up to date to mitigate potential vulnerabilities.

Troubleshooting kernel linking issues can be complex due to the low-level nature of kernel work. Kernel developers must be well-versed in using diagnostic tools like `dmesg` to inspect kernel logs for error messages related to module loading and symbol resolution. Such logs provide essential insights into issues that may arise during the linking process, signaling to developers where the problems lie and helping to expedite debugging efforts.

Kernel-level linking opens avenues for customization and optimization that developers can harness to their advantage. Understanding how linking operates at the kernel level allows developers to create efficient, high-performing, and secure applications that interact seamlessly with the operating system. As virtualization and containerization trends continue to evolve, the significance of kernel-level linking will likely increase, requiring developers to adapt their linking strategies to ensure compatibility and performance.

In summary, linking directly within the kernel is a powerful approach that requires careful consideration of performance, security, and complexity. Developers must remain vigilant regarding the intricacies of loadable modules, symbol visibility, and efficient linking practices. By mastering these elements, they can leverage kernel-level linking to create robust, high-performing applications capable of exploiting the full potential of the Linux operating system. With ongoing advancements in technology, the role of kernel linking will continue to evolve, underscoring its critical importance in modern software engineering.

16.3. Security Considerations in Kernel Linking

In the context of kernel linking, the security implications are profound but often overlooked in the broader discussion of software linking practices. By ensuring robust security measures when linking kernel modules and libraries, developers and system administrators can prevent vulnerabilities that could compromise entire systems. This section delves into key security considerations for kernel-level linking, outlining best practices to safeguard against threats.

Firstly, the importance of using only trusted libraries and modules cannot be overstated. The kernel serves as the core of the operating system, meaning any vulnerabilities in linked components can have severe consequences. Developers should ensure that all libraries and modules integrated into kernel space come from reputable sources, preferably those that are actively maintained and have established security protocols. Engaging with community-driven projects through platforms that emphasize best practices can help identify trustworthy libraries.

Another critical aspect of security involves memory management in linked modules. Kernel-level linking often requires managing dynamic memory allocation, which can lead to vulnerabilities such as buffer overflows. A common best practice in this regard is the use of static analysis tools during the development and testing phases. These tools can help identify potential issues in memory management even before the module is integrated into the kernel, reducing the chances of exploitation. Tools such as `clang` static analyzer can catch an array of bugs related to linking and memory misuse, allowing developers to address them proactively.

Moreover, implementing rigorous testing protocols is essential for ensuring the safety of linked modules. Comprehensive testing frameworks should be in place to validate the functionality of linked components under varying conditions. Creating test cases that cover edge scenarios and unexpected inputs can help expose weaknesses in the linking process, allowing developers to shore up those vulnerabilities before deployment.

Ensuring that kernel modules are signed helps to enhance security. Loadable kernel modules can be signed with cryptographic techniques, enabling the kernel to verify their integrity before loading them into memory. This method ensures that only approved modules are linked with the kernel, protecting against the risk of loading malicious code. The usage of module signatures is particularly important in environments where systems may be exposed to untrusted inputs, such as IoT devices or public cloud environments.

Given that kernel-level functions are accessible throughout the operating system, enforcing strict access controls on linked libraries is also vital. This includes defining which parts of the kernel can access specific libraries and ensuring that permissions are appropriately set. By adhering to the principle of least privilege, developers can minimize the potential impact of any vulnerabilities within linked libraries.

As vulnerabilities are discovered and patched in linked libraries, developers must have a systematic approach to updating those libraries while maintaining stability within the kernel. Establishing a routine for checking dependencies against known vulnerabilities is essential for proactive management. Tools such as OWASP Dependency-Check can help facilitate this monitoring process, providing alerts when vulnerabilities are identified within libraries or modules used in kernel-level linking.

Another critical aspect involves logging and monitoring efforts. Implementing robust logging mechanisms that track the operation of linked kernel modules can greatly aid in identifying anomalies. Should an attack occur or an unexpected behavior manifest, detailed logs help trace back the actions leading to the event, enabling response teams to take appropriate measures swiftly.

Lastly, community engagement plays a vital role in enhancing security within kernel linking. Developers should actively participate in open-source communities focused on kernel development, sharing insights and discussing best practices regarding security. Participating in forums can help uncover potential blind spots and vulnerabilities others have encountered, fostering a culture of learning and improvement.

In summary, the security considerations in kernel linking require developers to adopt multifaceted strategies encompassing cautious library selection, rigorous testing, memory management vigilance, cryptographic signing of modules, access control protocols, systematic monitoring for vulnerabilities, and community engagement. By implementing these best practices, developers can effectively mitigate risks, ensuring the security and integrity of the kernel and the applications that depend on it. As the landscape of software development continues to evolve, maintaining a proactive security posture in kernel linking will remain essential for safeguarding systems against emerging threats.

16.4. Performance Tuning Kernel Links

In the context of performance tuning kernel links, it is vital to recognize that kernel-level linking has a profound influence on system efficiency, especially as applications grow increasingly complex and resource-intensive. Performance tuning refers to the process of optimizing the linking of libraries and kernel modules to achieve the best possible execution speed, system responsiveness, and overall resource utilization. This is particularly relevant in high-performance computing environments, embedded systems, and real-time applications, where efficient linking practices can lead to significant gains in performance.

One of the primary strategies for performance tuning kernel links involves minimizing the overhead associated with symbol resolution. When the operating system kernel loads modules or libraries, it must resolve symbols—essentially, the functions and variables defined in those components. Reducing the number of symbols that require resolution during runtime can lead to performance improvements. Techniques such as dead code elimination—removing unused symbols from libraries—can help streamline the linking process. Developers can utilize tools like linker scripts to control which symbols are exported from modules, maintaining only essential functions that will be used in execution.

Another critical aspect of performance tuning is the careful management of memory allocation for linked libraries. Kernel modules often require precise control over memory usage, which can be achieved through optimized memory management practices. Developers should ensure that memory allocations are efficient, possibly employing strategies such as preallocating memory pools or using object allocators to minimize fragmentation. By controlling how memory is managed within linked modules, developers can enhance performance by reducing the overhead associated with dynamic memory allocation during execution.

Additionally, employing link-time optimization (LTO) provides the kernel with a holistic view of the application, allowing for cross-module optimizations that can lead to more efficient binaries. By considering the entire program's structure during the linking phase, the compiler can optimize critical execution paths and reduce the number of unnecessary function calls, thus enhancing performance. Using the -flto option when compiling modules can enable LTO, providing considerable improvements in execution speed for linked applications.

Precise control over the order of library linking can also play a role in enhancing performance. By carefully structuring the linking order in relation to dependency graphs, developers can facilitate better cache hit rates and reduce the need for costly memory accesses. Understanding locality of reference—accessing data that is located close together in memory—can lead to optimizations that minimize delays when fetching data required by linked libraries. Utilizing linker scripts to specify ordering or regions can be particularly effective in this regard.

Another performance tuning strategy involves leveraging lazy loading techniques when linking libraries. This approach requires libraries to be loaded into memory only when their functions are explicitly called. By postponing the loading of non-essential libraries, developers can reduce the memory footprint of applications during startup and conserve resources, leading to improved execution times in environments where performance is critical.

Implementing effective caching mechanisms can also enhance the performance of kernel links. Caching can minimize repeated resolution of symbols and reduce redundant access to shared libraries, speeding up execution times across the application. By linking against libraries that support caching, or creating custom caching solutions tailored to application use cases, developers can improve the responsiveness of linked applications significantly.

Performance monitoring and profiling tools are also indispensable in tuning kernel links. Using tools such as `perf`, `gprof`, or `strace`, developers can identify bottlenecks related to linked libraries and ascertain how modifications to linking strategies affect execution performance. Continuous profiling during development helps ensure that performance remains a focus as code evolves, aligning with the goal of maximizing efficiency in kernel-linked applications.

Lastly, establishing a culture of iterative testing and feedback can lead to continuous improvement in kernel linking processes. By maintaining a rigorous testing strategy that evaluates performance before and after linking adjustments, developers can ascertain the effectiveness of their tuning efforts. Using automated performance tests can streamline this process and allow developers to quickly identify any regressions resulting from changes.

In conclusion, performance tuning kernel links is paramount for achieving maximum efficiency within Linux applications. Through techniques that minimize symbol resolution overhead, optimize memory management, employ link-time optimizations, control the order of linking, utilize lazy loading, implement caching mechanisms, leverage performance profiling tools, and encourage iterative testing, developers can ensure that their applications achieve the desired speed and responsiveness. As applications continue to evolve, maintaining a performance-oriented mindset will be essential for leveraging the full capabilities of kernel-level linking in increasingly complex systems.

17. Linking in Real-Time Systems

17.1. Understanding Real-Time Systems

Understanding real-time systems within the context of linking practices is paramount for developers engaged in creating applications where timing and predictability are critical. Real-time systems are designed to respond to inputs within stringent deadlines, making them essential in scenarios such as aerospace, automotive control, medical devices, and telecommunications. The inherent requirements of these systems dictate distinct linking strategies to ensure the applications are not only functional but also responsive and reliable.

Real-time systems can be categorized into two primary types: hard real-time systems and soft real-time systems. Hard real-time systems require that critical tasks must be completed within specific time constraints without exception; failure to do so could result in catastrophic failures or dangerous consequences. Soft real-time systems, while still time-sensitive, are more lenient in that occasional delays might be tolerable without dire consequences. Understanding these classifications influences how developers approach linking in terms of prioritizing efficiency, resource usage, and response times.

When it comes to linking within real-time systems, the choice between static and dynamic linking becomes a crucial consideration. Static linking, where libraries are embedded into the final executable at compile time, can lead to predictable execution times because all necessary code is available immediately. This predictability aligns with the constraints of hard real-time systems, where ensuring that the application has quick access to all necessary functionalities is paramount.

Conversely, dynamic linking, where libraries are loaded at runtime, introduces the potential for variability in execution times, which can be detrimental in hard real-time systems. The overhead introduced by loading libraries and resolving symbols on-the-fly can lead to unpredictable delays that compromise the system's ability to meet deadlines. Gentle care must be taken if dynamic linking is utilized, ensuring that only essential libraries are included and that they are designed for low-latency interactions.

Another core aspect of linking in real-time systems involves optimizing memory usage. Given that real-time applications often operate in environments with limited resources, careful management of memory allocation becomes critical. Developers should minimize memory fragmentation since this can lead to unpredictable delays. Using techniques such as preallocating memory pools or choosing libraries that are optimized for memory use helps mitigate these risks, leading to more reliable performance.

Performance tuning is an ongoing requirement for real-time applications. Developers should utilize profiling tools to assess how libraries interact and execute, determining which functions are critical for performance. Techniques such as link-time optimization (LTO) should be considered, as they can help reduce unnecessary overhead by optimizing execution paths across multiple modules at the linking phase.

Furthermore, robustness in error handling is essential for real-time systems. Effective linking practices should enable rapid recovery from failures, whether due to library errors, symbol resolution failures, or other issues. Implementing strategies such as fallback mechanisms or gracefully degrading functionality in the event of failures helps maintain overall system performance and user experience.

Security considerations are paramount when linking libraries in real-time systems. The consequences of a compromised library could impact safety-critical operations, resulting in dire repercussions. By ensuring that only trusted libraries are linked, employing cryptographic signing and validation checks, and routinely monitoring libraries for vulnerabilities, developers can mitigate risks and enhance the security posture of their applications.

Testing practices tailored for real-time systems are equally vital. Rigorous testing must evaluate not only the correctness of linked libraries but also their performance dynamics under load. Stress testing and simulations that replicate real-world scenarios should be integral components of the testing process, ensuring that the application can perform within the necessary time constraints.

Innovations in real-time integration, as well as advancements in linking methodologies, provide developers with new opportunities to enhance their application's efficiency. Technologies that support real-time data processing and communication, such as real-time operating systems (RTOS) and specialized scheduling algorithms, are evolving to offer enhanced linking practices. The integration of such technologies into the development process can lead to improved response times and overall application performance.

In conclusion, understanding real-time systems and their implications for linking practices is essential for developers working within environments that demand reliability and timing. By employing careful strategies for static versus dynamic linking, optimizing memory usage, ensuring robust error handling, prioritizing security, and leveraging advanced performance tuning, developers can create real-time applications that meet stringent requirements and thrive within the Linux ecosystem. The future of linking in real-time systems will continue to evolve as developers embrace innovative technologies, deepen their understanding of timing constraints, and prioritize optimal outcomes for their applications.

17.2. Linking Techniques for Real-Time Applications

Linking techniques for real-time applications demand a specialized approach considering the stringent requirements and unique constraints of real-time systems. Real-time applications, from autopilot systems in aviation to critical medical devices, must guarantee timely execution, reliability, and performance. The linking process directly influences these factors, necessitating that developers adopt strategies designed to optimize application responsiveness while ensuring that linked libraries align with the operational demands inherent in real-time systems.

One of the fundamental strategies is the careful selection between static and dynamic linking. Static linking, where libraries are compiled directly into the final executable, is generally preferred in real-time applications for its predictability. Since all required code resides within the executable itself, the system can avoid the potential delays associated with dynamic linking, where libraries are loaded during runtime, requiring real-time applications to resolve symbols at unpredictable intervals. For instance, in a hard real-time automotive control system, static linking ensures that the code paths remain consistent and time-sensitive functions execute without delay.

However, static linking can lead to larger binaries, which might not be suitable for all real-time applications, especially those deployed on resource-constrained embedded systems. Additionally, static linking ties the application tightly to the linked library versions, potentially complicating updates. As such, developers must evaluate their specific use cases carefully. If dynamic linking must be used, it is vital to ensure that the libraries are optimized for low-latency execution and that the overall design anticipates the added overhead.

In conjunction with the linking type, memory management optimization is essential. Real-time applications often operate within environments with limited RAM and processing power. Developers can employ techniques such as memory pooling, allocating fixed-size blocks of memory for frequently-used objects, to minimize fragmentation and ensure that allocated resources are promptly available. Additionally, using lightweight libraries that provide the necessary functionalities without excessive overhead can further enhance resource utilization.

Performance tuning also plays an instrumental role in ensuring timely execution within real-time applications. Incorporating profiling tools can provide developers with insights into how functions interact and identify bottlenecks, facilitating targeted optimization efforts. Tools such as `perf` and `gprof` can be invaluable, allowing engineers to fine-tune critical segments of linked libraries to guarantee they meet real-time performance standards.

Fault tolerance mechanisms must be embedded within the linking strategies. In the event that a linked library fails or encounters an error, the system should have defined recovery procedures. Implementing redundancy strategies or fallbacks can ensure that the application continues to operate correctly, even if a specific library fails to load. Implementing these mechanisms during the linking phase can provide peace of mind, knowing that linked libraries do not jeopardize the application's integrity under failure conditions.

Security becomes a pivotal concern when linking for real-time applications. The ramifications of vulnerabilities in linked libraries can be particularly severe in safety-critical scenarios, where errors can lead to catastrophic failures. Developers must be diligent about selecting trusted libraries and regularly applying updates to mitigate risks stemming from known vulnerabilities. Careful scrutiny of third-party libraries used in real-time applications is essential, ensuring that they comply with the latest security protocols and practices.

Lastly, effective testing and validation processes tailored for real-time applications are necessary. Rigorous performance testing should ensure that linked libraries function as expected under load, and real-world conditions are simulated to reveal any potential timing issues. Comprehensive test suites that address functional requirements alongside timing constraints are crucial for maintaining operational reliability.

In summary, espousing best practices in linking techniques for real-time applications centers on careful consideration of static versus dynamic linking, optimization of memory management, performance tuning, integrating fault tolerance mechanisms, ensuring library security, and conducting thorough testing. By implementing these strategies, developers can create robust, efficient real-time applications that respond predictably to user interactions and external conditions.

17.3. Advancements in Real-Time Integration

In recent years, advancements in real-time integration for linking practices in the Linux ecosystem have increasingly garnered attention. As applications continue to grow in complexity and interconnectivity, the demands placed upon real-time systems have spurred innovation in how developers approach linking libraries and modules for optimal performance under strict timing constraints. One prominent advancement is the development of low-latency communication protocols that optimize how libraries interface within real-time applications. Protocols such as Real Time Messaging Protocol (RTMP) and Lightweight Messaging Protocol (LwM2M) enhance the efficiency of data transfer between linked components, minimizing overhead and ensuring timely execution.

Additionally, improvements in scheduling algorithms have emerged as critical to real-time integration. The integration of advanced scheduling techniques, such as Rate Monotonic Scheduling (RMS) and Earliest Deadline First (EDF), helps manage resources effectively and prioritize critical tasks. These algorithms work in conjunction with linked library functions to ensure that important processes are dispatched on time and execute as expected, enabling real-time applications to meet stringent performance requirements.

Another key area of advancement lies in the optimization of linking techniques through Just-In-Time (JIT) compilation. JIT compilers can dynamically generate native code at runtime, which is particularly beneficial for just-in-time resolution of libraries and functions that are time-sensitive. By strategically compiling and linking code snippets that are invoked frequently, developers can significantly reduce execution times and enhance the performance of real-time systems.

Furthermore, advancements in distributed computing have influenced real-time integration through microservices architectures. This approach allows for the decomposition of applications into smaller, independent services linked through APIs, promoting flexibility and adaptability in real-time applications. Each microservice can be linked with lightweight libraries tailored to its specific functionality, resulting in improved performance and responsiveness in real-time operations.

In tandem with these technological advancements, the push for collaborative development practices has fostered the creation of community-driven libraries focused on real-time applications. These libraries are continuously refined and optimized through the contributions of developers who share a common interest in advancing real-time capabilities. Engaging with these communities enables developers to adopt best practices and benefit from collective insights, driving further innovation in linking strategies.

As real-time systems increasingly integrate with technologies like Edge Computing and the Internet of Things (IoT), the methodologies surrounding linking practices are likely to evolve even more. Real-time systems will need to remain agile and adaptable, capable of delivering timely performance while navigating complex networks of interconnected devices. The future of real-time integration in linking practices within the Linux ecosystem promises to enhance operational efficacy, ushering in a new era of performance-driven software solutions.

In summary, the advancements in real-time integration for linking practices embody the intersection of innovation, community collaboration, and evolving methodologies. By leveraging developments in low-latency protocols, advanced scheduling techniques, JIT compilation, microservices architectures, and collaborative library development, developers can ensure that real-time applications perform optimally within the interconnected landscape of modern computing. Embracing these advancements will be essential for meeting the ever-growing demands of real-time systems in an evolving technological world, ultimately enriching the Linux ecosystem as a whole.

17.4. Troubleshooting Real-Time Link Failures

Troubleshooting Real-Time Link Failures is a crucial aspect of ensuring the reliability and responsiveness of applications that operate within strict timing constraints, such as those found in real-time systems. When linked libraries and components fail to work as expected, the repercussions can be severe—leading to system failures, degraded performance, or even safety hazards in critical applications. Understanding common issues that can arise during the linking process, along with effective diagnostic and resolution strategies, is essential for developers and engineers working in this space.

One prevalent issue encountered in real-time link failures is symbol resolution errors. This occurs when the linker cannot find the necessary symbols defined in the linked libraries, typically because of mismatched versions or missed dependencies. For example, if a library function that is expected by the application has been removed in a newer version of the library, the linker will generate an error. To troubleshoot this, developers must ensure that all linked libraries are compatible with each other and that the application is aware of the correct versions. A thorough examination of the linking command and associated flags can help identify where the linkage may have failed. Tools like ldd or examining the link output in detail can provide insights into the expected versus actual library dependencies.

Another common problem can occur during dynamic linking, where libraries are loaded at runtime. If a necessary library is not available in the system path, the application may fail to start or crash unexpectedly. To mitigate this, developers can set the LD_LIBRARY_PATH environment variable appropriately, adding directories containing dependent libraries to ensure they're accessible when the application executes. Verifying the deployment environment for any missing libraries or incorrect library versions is essential for a successful linking operation, especially in real-time contexts where applications must be consistently responsive.

Configuration issues—where incorrect paths to libraries are specified —can also lead to linking failures. These issues become more prominent when applications are moved between environments, such as during development and production versions. Developers should implement configuration management solutions that maintain consistent references to library locations and use relative paths when possible to avoid hard-coded issues introduced by different environments.

Memory management issues can disproportionately affect linked real-time applications. When an application dynamically allocates memory for linked libraries but fails to manage that memory adequately, it can lead to memory leaks or fragmentation. Employing tools like Valgrind can aid in identifying these issues during the testing phase, allowing developers to optimize memory usage and avoid real-time failures due to resource exhaustion.

Linking to incompatible libraries can also produce runtime failures in real-time applications. There are often cases where multiple projects rely on varying versions of the same library, leading to conflicts. A useful practice is to leverage containerization or virtual environments which encapsulate the application and its libraries, ensuring that each environment operates with its intended versions. This can alleviate many linking conflicts that arise from version discrepancies across systems.

Debugging linked libraries within real-time applications can be challenging due to the performance overhead added by tools. However, using lightweight debugging tools like GDB can be effective. Developers should familiarize themselves with effective debugging techniques to step through linked code and pinpoint the source of failures in real-time operations. Implementing logging mechanisms that track library calls and errors can also help in diagnosing issues when they arise during execution.

Security vulnerabilities introduced through linked libraries are an additional concern, particularly in applications operating in mission-critical environments. Developers should stay abreast of known vulnerabilities in the libraries used and be proactive in applying updates, employing automated vulnerability scanning tools when necessary. Implementing security measures during the linking process, such as using signed libraries, can help ensure the integrity of the linked components and mitigate the risk of exploitation.

In conclusion, troubleshooting real-time link failures in applications requires a multidimensional approach that encompasses a thorough understanding of the linking process, effective diagnostic strategies, and an emphasis on stability, memory management, and security. By focusing on common issues related to symbol resolution, environment management, memory optimization, and dependency conflicts, developers can enhance the reliability and performance of their real-time applications, ensuring they can meet the stringent requirements of their operational environments. Consistent testing, monitoring, and community engagement will fortify practices around linking in real-time systems, leading to better outcomes and more resilient applications.

18. Legal and Ethical Considerations in Software Linking

18.1. Licensing Considerations for Libraries

In today's software development landscape, linking considerations play a vital role in how libraries are managed and utilized within various contexts, particularly in libraries utilized by libraries in libraries. For libraries, understanding the particular issues surrounding licensing and ethics not only streamlines development processes but also fosters a collaborative and respectful environment amongst developers and organizations. This subchapter focuses on the critical aspects of licensing considerations for libraries, examining the legal stipulations and ethical implications tied to linking practices in the Linux ecosystem.

Licensing is a pivotal factor in how libraries can be utilized within applications. Each library typically comes with its specific licensing framework, stipulating the terms and conditions under which it can be used, modified, and shared. Developers must familiarize themselves with these licenses to ensure compliance when linking libraries in their applications. Common open-source licenses, such as the GNU General Public License (GPL), MIT License, and Apache License, exhibit different requirements, particularly concerning derivative works and distribution.

For instance, the GPL requires that if an application links against a library licensed under GPL, then the entire application must also be made available under the same GPL license when distributed. This requirement can have significant implications for developers looking to monetize their applications or maintain proprietary control, as it mandates the release of source code associated with the application. Conversely, licenses such as the MIT License or Apache License allow for greater flexibility, permitting developers to link against libraries without imposing the same restrictions on their own code. Understanding these nuances is critical for developers to align their linking practices with their project goals.

Another crucial aspect of licensing considerations involves dependency management. In complex applications, developers often rely on multiple libraries, each with its licensing terms. The interaction between these licenses can create compliance challenges. For example, if an application links against a GPL library and also includes libraries under more permissive licenses, the overall licensing requirements could shift, potentially subjecting the entire project to GPL conditions. Developers must actively assess their libraries' licenses in the context of their cumulative impact, ensuring that all components are compatible and do not introduce conflicts.

Ethical considerations also play a significant role in the responsible management of libraries. This includes recognizing the contributions of library authors and maintainers. When using external libraries, developers should ensure proper attribution in accordance with the license guidelines. While open-source licenses promote sharing and contribution, they also place the onus of respecting the original authors' work on developers. Respecting the intent behind licenses supports a healthy ecosystem that encourages collaboration among developers, fosters innovation, and enhances the overall quality of open-source projects.

Additionally, developers seeking to create their libraries should remain cognizant of ethical practices as they design, document, and license their work. They must strive to produce well-documented libraries that offer clear usage instructions and actively encourage contributions while avoiding potentially restrictive licensing. By adopting ethical considerations throughout library development, developers contribute to the creation of a supportive and collaborative community.

Community contributions to open-source projects are part of a broader ethos that enhances the quality of software ecosystems. When contributing to community-driven projects or libraries, developers should take the time to understand the existing practices and guidelines that govern contributions. This includes adhering to the established code of conduct, participating in discussions, submitting high-quality pull requests, and ensuring that contributions are aligned with the project's licensing.

Avoiding common pitfalls in linking requires an awareness of both legal and ethical considerations. For example, developers should not use libraries with incompatible licenses with the intent to form a combined work without adequate understanding of how the linked licenses interact. Engaging with legal experts or utilizing resources that clarify licensing complexities could help developers navigate these murky waters. Additionally, respecting the wishes of the community by maintaining proper documentation, code attributions, and adhering to open-source ethics increases the overall integrity and reliability of software development efforts. Not only does this foster trust in community interactions, but it also enhances the reputation of developers within the ecosystem.

In conclusion, licensing considerations for libraries represent a critical aspect of linking practices in software development. Developers must remain vigilant in understanding the legal stipulations tied to libraries they utilize, ensuring compliance with various licenses while also upholding ethical practices in acknowledgment of original authors' work. By fostering collaborative relationships within the community, adhering to licensing guidelines, and respecting contributions, developers can create a richer, more sustainable open-source ecosystem that continues to thrive in the digital age. Emphasizing these principles will help developers not only navigate the intricacies of linking but also contribute to a respectful and innovative software landscape.

18.2. Ethics in Open Source Development

Ethics in Open Source Development

In the world of software development, particularly within the realm of open source, ethical considerations are paramount. As numerous developers, organizations, and communities engage with and contribute to open source projects, a shared understanding of ethical practices becomes increasingly vital. Open source is not merely a technical approach; it is underpinned by principles that emphasize collaboration, transparency, respect, and responsibility. This chapter highlights key ethical considerations in open-source development, particularly in relation to linking practices, to ensure that developers contribute positively to the community and promote sustainable software practices.

One of the foundational principles of open source ethics is the commitment to transparency. Developers who contribute to open source projects are expected to be open about their intentions, methodologies, and the implications of their contributions. This transparency extends to documenting code, outlining the functionality of libraries, and providing licenses that clearly stipulate how the code can be used. By adhering to transparent practices, developers foster trust within the community, enabling others to understand and improve upon what has been created.

Additionally, appreciation for the original authors of libraries and code bases is essential in maintaining an ethical framework. When using or incorporating third-party libraries, developers should provide proper attribution in accordance with their licenses. Acknowledging the contributions of authors not only respects their work but also supports a culture of collaboration and mutual respect that is intrinsic to the open-source community. It is vital for developers to grasp the licensing terms associated with each library they utilize and ensure they comply fully while providing appropriate credit.

Another ethical consideration concerns the quality and integrity of code contributed to open source projects. As developers submit code or libraries for inclusion in open source projects, they must prioritize producing high-quality work that adheres to best practices. This includes thoroughly testing their code, maintaining clear documentation, and following established coding standards. By doing so, developers contribute to the overall health of the project and enhance the experience for all who use it. Conversely, contributing poorly written or untested code can create complications for the project and harm its reputation.

The spirit of collaboration is a central tenet of open source development ethics, and developers should strive to foster inclusive and constructive environments within communities. This encompasses being open to feedback, encouraging diverse perspectives, and prioritizing respectful interactions in discussions. Developers are encouraged to engage with others in a manner that prioritizes dialogue over confrontation, understanding that differing viewpoints can lead to stronger outcomes. This collaborative mindset is essential for encouraging new contributors while also helping to avoid divisiveness within the community.

When contributing to or using open-source software, ethical developers also consider the implications of their actions on the community, including the potential for misuse of code or libraries. Developers should always be vigilant about how the software they contribute might be used, ensuring they do not contribute to projects or libraries that could lead to harmful outcomes, whether that involves security vulnerabilities, unethical applications, or actions that could endanger users' privacy. Ethical considerations compel developers to exercise due diligence in their contributions, ultimately promoting the concept of responsible software development.

Furthermore, it is essential for developers to remain engaged with the community as it evolves. Open-source projects are inherently dynamic, and staying updated about the direction, challenges, and needs of the community can inform ethical decision-making. Participating in discussions, contributing actively, and sharing knowledge helps foster a healthy ecosystem and can enable developers to identify ethical concerns as they arise.

Finally, education plays a crucial role in nurturing ethical practices within the open-source community. Developers must strive to stay informed about best practices, legal considerations, and ethical implications related to licensing, contributions, and interactions within the community. Engaging with resources—from workshops and conferences to online courses—can enhance understanding and support ethical engagement with open-source projects.

In summary, ethics in open source development is a multifaceted consideration encompassing transparency, attribution, code quality, collaboration, responsible usage, and community engagement. By cultivating an ethical framework, developers not only uphold the principles that define open source but also promote a positive and inclusive environment that benefits the entirety of the software development community. Emphasizing these ethical considerations ensures that the rich legacy of open source development continues to thrive, as developers harness the power of collaboration to build innovative and high-quality software solutions.

18.3. Community Contributions and You

In the evolving landscape of software development, the significance of community contributions in open-source projects, especially regarding linking practices, cannot be understated. As a developer, engaging with the open-source community not only promotes collaboration and innovation but also allows you to foster a supportive and inclusive environment that benefits everyone involved. This aspect of development involves not just code contributions, but also participation in discussions, sharing knowledge, and taking part in initiatives that focus on shared goals. This subchapter examines how you can contribute responsibly to community-driven projects while enhancing your skills and building meaningful networks.

One of the first steps in engaging with the community is to familiarize yourself with the project's contribution guidelines. These guidelines are typically outlined in the project's repository, often in a file named CONTRIBUTING.md. They provide essential information on the process for contributing code, reporting issues, and best practices for using the project. Understanding these rules is crucial to avoid frustration and ensure your contributions are well received. If the guidelines are vague or the project lacks them, reach out to other community members for clarification.

When contributing code or libraries to a project, it's vital to adhere to coding standards that maintain the quality and readability of the codebase. Review existing code to understand the style and conventions employed within the project. By following established coding practices, you contribute to a cohesive and manageable codebase, which benefits other contributors and developers who will work with the project in the future. Additionally, thorough documentation of your code, including comments that clarify its purpose and use, is essential for ensuring future maintainers understand your contributions.

Collaborating effectively is a cornerstone of successful community contributions. This involves being open to feedback and discussions regarding your code changes. When submitting pull requests, engage in conversations about the changes you've made and be receptive to suggestions for improvement. Open communication fosters a sense of camaraderie, encouraging others to provide constructive responses and ensuring that your contributions align with the project's overall goals.

Consider expanding your contribution efforts beyond code. Get involved in documentation or educational resources that help new users get acclimated to the project. High-quality documentation enhances user experience and contributes significantly to the sustainability of the project. Also, helping others on community forums can cement your role as a supportive community member, creating relationships that benefit your learning and growth.

Fostering an inclusive environment is also instrumental in community contributions. Emphasizing diversity and equity within the community not only promotes better ideas and innovations, but also enriches the project. Encourage and mentor newcomers by providing guidance and knowledge, actively participating in discussions that support inclusive practices, and adhering to codes of conduct that maintain respect and openness. A welcoming atmosphere encourages others to contribute their unique perspectives and skills.

As you engage with the community, remember that sharing what you learn is just as valuable as your code contributions. Blog posts, online articles, and talks at local meetups about your experiences and insights can help others while enhancing your own understanding. Teaching and sharing knowledge cements your status as a committed community member and contributes to the collective knowledge base of the community.

Another important consideration in contributing to the community is maintaining awareness of the legal and ethical aspects of software licensing. Understanding the implications of the licenses associated with the libraries you utilize or contribute to is critical for both compliance and ethical usage. Engage with relevant discussions surrounding library licenses, understand their terms, and ensure that your contributions uphold these principles.

Lastly, recognizing that community contributions may not always result in immediate acknowledgment or acceptance is part of the journey. Open-source projects often have distinct flows and timelines that may influence feedback. Use such experiences as learning opportunities to refine your skills and adapt your contributions for future iterations.

In conclusion, contributing responsibly to community-driven projects involves engaging with the community through meaningful and respectful collaboration, adhering to coding standards, understanding licensing, and remaining receptive to feedback. By fostering an inclusive atmosphere, sharing knowledge, and contributing to various aspects of the project, you empower both your professional growth and the collective advancement of the open-source community. Embracing these principles enriches your experience as a developer and reinforces the values that underpin successful community contributions.

18.4. Avoiding Common Pitfalls in Linking

As developers engage with libraries and linking in their projects, understanding how to avoid common pitfalls is crucial for creating reliable software. This section discusses practical advice to help navigate these challenges.

One of the primary mistakes developers make is neglecting to fully understand the licensing implications of the libraries they use. Different libraries have various licenses — some may require that any derivative work also be open-source, while others may allow proprietary use. Failing to adhere to these terms can lead to legal consequences or a loss of trust within the community. Before integrating a library, thoroughly read the license and assess how it aligns with your project goals. Use tools that can automatically check dependencies and their licenses for compliance.

Another common pitfall involves poorly managing library versions. Projects that depend on multiple libraries can face challenges if one library undergoes significant changes or updates. This can result in conflicts and bugs that can derail development. To mitigate this, implement strict version control — use dependency management tools that lock specific versions of libraries. This allows continued stability as individual libraries can be updated minimally or as needed rather than having everything update at once.

Improperly testing linked libraries can also lead to significant issues. It's crucial to have a comprehensive testing framework that includes unit tests, integration tests, and regression tests. Automated tests should be part of the CI/CD pipeline to ensure that any changes in libraries do not introduce new errors. Neglecting testing may result in unforeseen issues during production, and having robust tests in place will ultimately save time and effort when debugging.

Additionally, developers often overlook the importance of documenting their linking process. Clarity about which libraries are used, their versions, and how they are linked within the application can help others (and future you) understand the project's structure. Proper documentation alleviates confusion and makes onboarding new team members easier. It's advisable to maintain a dedicated file or set of comments in the codebase that captures this information.

Security vulnerabilities are another area where common pitfalls can occur. Libraries often contain known vulnerabilities that can expose applications to exploits. Regularly assessing libraries using automated tools to scan for vulnerabilities and applying updates promptly is essential for maintaining security. Additionally, adopt best practices such as removing unused dependencies that can introduce potential risks to the application.

Networking and communication within the development community can be helpful in avoiding pitfalls. Engaging with forums, attending workshops, or joining local developer groups allows access to shared experiences and knowledge. Ask others about their experiences when linking various libraries, what pitfalls they encountered, and the solutions they implemented.

Lastly, adapting to the evolving landscape of tools and practices is essential. The software development field is always advancing, with new tools and languages emerging. Continuous learning through courses, reading, and participating in conferences ensures that developers are equipped to avoid common pitfalls and stay ahead of any potential issues in linking practices.

In summary, to avoid common pitfalls in linking, developers should focus on understanding licensing, managing library versions strategically, implementing comprehensive testing practices, maintaining thorough documentation, ensuring security through vulnerability management, engaging with the community, and committing to ongoing learning. These strategies collectively enhance the reliability and quality of software applications linked through libraries in the Linux ecosystem.

19. Resources and Continued Learning

19.1. Companion Technologies and Tools

In today's tech-savvy world, developers rely heavily on various companion technologies and tools that complement and enhance the linking practices associated with libraries in the Linux ecosystem. Understanding and utilizing these auxiliary tools can significantly streamline the development process, improve application performance, and facilitate debugging and maintenance of linked applications. This section explores a diverse array of technologies and tools developers should consider incorporating into their workflows to optimize linking strategies and enhance the overall software development lifecycle.

One of the fundamental technologies that supports effective linking practices is the GNU Compiler Collection (GCC). GCC not only serves as a powerful compiler for various programming languages but also offers robust linking capabilities. Its flexibility enables developers to utilize multiple options such as link-time optimization (LTO) and integration with linker scripts. As a companion tool in the linking process, GCC empowers developers to compile and link with high efficiency while managing dependencies effectively.

Another key tool is CMake, a widely used cross-platform build system that simplifies the process of managing complex builds. CMake automates the generation of makefiles, ensuring that the appropriate linking commands are generated based on the specified project configurations. This tool enhances collaboration, as it accommodates various development environments, making it easier for teams to share and integrate their codebases without conflict.

Autotools is another companion technology that automates the configuration and build process for software projects. It provides a set of tools for generating the `configure` script, which detects system features and enables developers to define options for compilation and linking. By ensuring that the right libraries are linked based on user environments, Autotools lays a solid foundation for consistent builds across different systems.

Additionally, testing frameworks such as Google Test for C++ and JUnit for Java play an essential role in supporting linked applications. Implementing automated unit and integration tests helps verify that linked libraries interact as intended and that no regressions are introduced after linking changes. Reliability in library linking can be significantly bolstered through these testing frameworks, providing developers with the confidence that their applications will perform consistently.

To monitor performance and analyze executables, profiling tools like `gprof`, `perf`, and Valgrind become invaluable companions in the development process. These tools enable developers to pinpoint bottlenecks in linked applications, allowing for targeted optimizations and ensuring that linked libraries deliver maximum performance without excess overhead. Continuous performance monitoring facilitates iterative improvements, ensuring that linking strategies evolve alongside the application's needs.

Speaking of community engagement, the Linux community serves as a rich resource for developers seeking to optimize their practices. Online forums, mailing lists, and collaborative platforms such as GitHub foster discussions on best practices for linking. The availability of tutorials, documentation, and novel approaches produces a vibrant ecosystem that continuously cultivates advancements in linking methodologies.

Moreover, resource management tools like Docker and Kubernetes have transformed how libraries are linked, especially in cloud-native development. Through containerization, these tools promote efficient linking practices that ensure a lean footprint while managing dependencies effectively. Developers can package applications with their libraries, eliminating concerns about version conflicts and making deployment straightforward.

Data serialization frameworks, such as Protocol Buffers, are also noteworthy companion tools. They facilitate efficient data exchange between linked libraries or microservices, complying with performance constraints in applications, particularly in distributed systems. By optimizing communication between libraries, they validate that linking practices preserve application responsiveness.

In summary, a comprehensive toolkit consisting of compilers, build systems, testing frameworks, profiling tools, community resources, data serialization frameworks, and resource management technologies serve as invaluable companions to link and manage libraries in Linux applications efficiently. By equipping themselves with these tools and fostering a culture of collaboration and continued learning, developers can enhance their linking practices, optimize performance, and ultimately deliver high-quality software solutions that meet the demands of an ever-evolving tech landscape. Embracing these companion technologies and tools will empower developers to push the boundaries of what is achievable through effective linking and library management in their applications.

19.2. Linux Community and Online Resources

The Linux community is a rich source of knowledge, support, and resources for developers and system administrators alike, particularly when it comes to understanding and mastering the intricacies of linking libraries within their applications. This subchapter will explore the various facets of the Linux community, outline online resources, and recommend avenues for continued learning to help you cultivate your skills in Linux linking.

One of the primary ways to engage with the Linux community is through online forums and discussion boards. Platforms like Stack Overflow and the LinuxQuestions.org forum are invaluable for obtaining answers to specific linking issues or broader queries related to library management. Here, developers can ask questions, share experiences, and collaborate with others who are facing similar challenges. Engaging with the community in these forums fosters problem-solving and deepens understanding of linking practices.

Social media groups, such as those on Reddit (r/linux, r/programming, or r/linux_gaming), can also provide a wealth of information. Not only can you find discussions related to linking practices, but you can also participate in conversations about best practices, industry trends, and emerging technologies. Following key figures in the Linux community on platforms like Twitter can keep you informed about notable news and updates regarding linking in Linux.

Documentation is another cornerstone of the Linux community. The official GNU documentation, available at the GNU Project's website, provides comprehensive guides on GCC, linker options, and advanced linking techniques, which are essential for developers seeking to deepen their understanding. Additionally, the man pages in Linux systems (man ld, man gcc) offer succinct information and practical examples, serving as a quick reference for linking commands and options directly from the terminal.

Open-source projects and repositories on platforms like GitHub host a trove of libraries and linking patterns that exemplify best practices. By exploring existing projects or contributing your own, you can learn from the code architecture and relevant linking strategies applied therein. Collaborating on open-source projects not only enhances your technical skills but also enables networking with other contributing developers who share similar interests.

For those seeking formal education and structured learning, a variety of online courses and resources are dedicated to Linux development and advanced programming concepts that cover linking. Websites like Coursera, edX, and Udacity offer courses focused on Linux programming, data structures, and algorithm design, often teaching concepts applicable to efficient linking. Consider courses from institutions such as Stanford University, MIT, or industry experts in these spaces.

Books dedicated to Linux system programming and development enrich knowledge on the subject matter. Highly recommended titles include "Linux Programming by Example" by Alan C. McClellan and

"Advanced Programming in the Unix Environment" by W. Richard Stevens. These texts provide insights into library management, linking practices, and effective use of system calls in Linux applications.

Industry conferences and workshops present excellent opportunities for networking and learning. Events like the Linux Foundation's Open Source Summit, PyCon for Python developers, or the Annual ACM Symposium on Operating Systems Principles offer workshops, sessions, and tutorials that delve into advanced topics, including linking in distributed applications or problem-solving linked library conflicts. Attending such events allows developers to stay abreast of the latest trends, engage with expert speakers, and form connections with peers in the industry.

Local user groups or meetups also play a significant role in fostering community around Linux and open-source technologies. These smaller gatherings allow for intimate discussions, hands-on workshops, and collaborative problem-solving around linking practices. Engaging in these groups, whether in person or virtually, can help cultivate your skills while building valuable relationships within the Linux community.

In summary, the Linux community serves as a robust resource for developers seeking to enhance their skills in linking libraries and managing dependencies. By engaging with online forums, utilizing comprehensive documentation, exploring open-source projects, participating in educational courses, reading relevant texts, and attending conferences, you can cultivate a deeper understanding of linking practices while becoming an active participant in the community. Leveraging these resources will empower you to troubleshoot effectively and contribute to the ongoing advancement of software development in the Linux environment.

19.3. Recommended Reading and Courses

Recommended Reading and Courses

To deepen your understanding of linking practices in Linux, as well as the broader concepts that surround the effective use of libraries, it is beneficial to explore a variety of resources that cater to different aspects of software development. Below is a curated selection of recommended reading materials and online courses that provide valuable insights into linking in Linux environments, optimizing performance, and maintaining best practices in software development.

Books:

1. "Linkers and Loaders" by John R. Levine - This book offers an in-depth look at the principles and functionality of linkers and loaders. Understanding these concepts can greatly enhance your knowledge of how linking operates at a low level, leading to better-designed applications.

2. "Advanced Programming in the Unix Environment" by W. Richard Stevens - A staple in system programming literature, this book covers various aspects of Unix-based systems, including detailed discussions on linking and using libraries effectively within application development.

3. "The Linux Programming Interface" by Michael Kerrisk - This comprehensive resource provides an extensive overview of the Linux API, including focused sections on library management, linking, and system calls. It is essential reading for developers looking to deepen their understanding of Linux internals.

4. "The Definitive Guide to Linux Network Programming" by Richard Stevens, Bill Fenner, and Andrew Rudoff - While primarily focused on networking, this book discusses various libraries used in networked applications and provides insights into linking practices that support efficient network communication.

5. "Linux System Programming" by Robert Love - This book details various system programming concepts in Linux, including file handling, process management, and linking libraries.

Online Courses:

1. Coursera: "Linux for Developers" - This course covers essential Linux skills, focusing on the command line, system calls, and

191

effective development practices on Linux, including library usage and linking.

2. edX: "Introduction to Linux" - Offered by The Linux Foundation, this course is a comprehensive introduction to Linux. While it covers the basics, topics related to system programming and library management are also addressed.

3. Udacity: "C++ Programming for Beginners" - This course provides a solid grounding in C++, guiding students through fundamental programming concepts including linking static and dynamic libraries. Though focused on C++, the principles are applicable across various coding languages.

4. Pluralsight: "Linux System Programming" - Aimed at intermediate developers, this course delves into the intricacies of system programming on Linux, focusing on libraries and linking practices.

5. LinkedIn Learning: "Learning Linux Command Line" - While not specifically about linking, this course equips developers with the Linux command line skills needed to manipulate files and run scripts that are often critical when working with libraries and linking.

Conferences and Workshops:

Attending industry events is an excellent way to expand your knowledge, network with other professionals, and stay updated on the latest trends in linking practices and software development methodologies. Here are some notable conferences and workshops you might consider:

1. LinuxCon - A premier convention dedicated to exploring the latest and greatest in Linux technologies, this conference gathers industry experts to provide insights into kernel developments, open-source libraries, and linking practices.

2. Open Source Summit - Hosted by The Linux Foundation, this summit focuses on diverse topics across the open-source landscape,

with sessions on library management, linking best practices, and security considerations.

3. PyCon - If you are a Python developer, PyCon is an ideal venue for learning about libraries and linking practices specific to Python applications, along with networking with other developers.

4. FOSDEM (Free and Open Source Software Developers' European Meeting) - This event offers tracks on various open-source topics, including sessions that cover linking libraries and best practices in multiple programming languages.

5. DevOps Days - This global series of conferences emphasizes combining development and operational practices, often addressing topics like containerization and efficient linking in cloud-based environments.

6. Local meetups - Many cities host local Linux user groups or meetups where developers gather to discuss specific topics, including linking practices. Check platforms like Meetup.com to find groups in your area.

In conclusion, leveraging these recommended reading materials, online courses, and industry events will enrich your understanding of linking in Linux environments and the effective management of libraries. Keeping abreast of new technologies and engaging with the community will undoubtedly enhance your skills and capacity to develop robust, high-performing applications that leverage best practices in linking methodologies.

19.4. Conferences and Workshops for Enthusiasts

In the tech landscape, conferences and workshops emerge as vital platforms for enthusiasts, developers, and professionals eager to expand their knowledge of linking practices, libraries, and the intricacies of Linux development. These gatherings offer opportunities for networking, collaboration, and immersion in the latest advancements, trends, and technologies while fostering a sense of community among like-minded individuals passionate about open-source software and contemporary development methodologies.

One of the leading conferences in this space is the Open Source Summit, hosted by The Linux Foundation. This multi-day event gathers experts and contributors from across the open-source ecosystem to share insights on a wide range of topics including linking practices, library management, and maintaining open-source projects. Participants can engage in hands-on workshops, attend technical sessions, and learn about the latest tools and trends impacting the industry. Engaging with peers and industry leaders provides invaluable takeaways, promoting collaborative innovation.

LinuxCon is another prestigious event focused specifically on Linux technologies. It features tracks dedicated to kernel development, practical linking strategies, and system programming insights. Attendees often include not just developers but also system administrators and project managers, making it an ideal venue for cross-disciplinary collaboration. Sessions often cover crucial topics such as dynamic linking, static linking strategies, and optimizing library usage, which can significantly influence application performance and behavior.

For those interested in the field of containerization, KubeCon + CloudNativeCon is a must-attend event that explores Kubernetes and cloud-native technologies that heavily rely on efficient linking of services. The workshops and talks emphasize best practices for ensuring seamless library integration in microservices architectures, addressing the challenges of dependency management at scale. The conference fosters cutting-edge discussions on how containerization affects linking techniques, performance, and scalability in cloud-native applications.

DevOpsDays is an excellent conference for those focused on the intersection of development and operations. Discussions surrounding continuous integration (CI) and continuous deployment (CD) practices often touch upon linking strategies and library management. Attending these conferences can provide insights into how linking practices that support operational efficiency and agile development methodologies can enhance overall software delivery.

Furthermore, specialized conferences or workshops, such as FOSDEM (Free and Open Source Software Developers' European Meeting), present a unique opportunity for developers. This event focuses on the vibrant open source community and includes discussions on library linking, maintenance practices, and ecosystem health. The diverse range of presentations encourages knowledge sharing and sparks collaborative initiatives among attendees.

In stricter language domains, PyCon is a leading conference for Python enthusiasts. It typically features sessions that explore Python's rich ecosystem of libraries and extensions, addressing linking practices pertinent to Python applications. This can be especially beneficial for developers interested in optimizing application performance and understanding how to efficiently manage dependencies in their Python projects.

Local Meetups also provide informal yet valuable opportunities for enthusiasts to gather, network, and learn from each other. Platforms like Meetup.com can facilitate access to communities of developers focused on Linux, open-source software, and specific programming languages. These gatherings often feature presentations, collaborative coding, and discussions surrounding the latest trends in linking and library management.

In addition to physical conferences, many organizations and communities host virtual workshops and webinars, allowing participants from around the globe to join discussions on linking practices and library management in real-time. These online events can be especially valuable for those who may not have access to local meetups or larger conferences.

In conclusion, conferences and workshops play a pivotal role in advancing knowledge, sharing innovations, and fostering collaboration among developers and enthusiasts in the Linux community. By attending these events, professionals can immerse themselves in the latest developments in linking technologies, network with peers, and strengthen their understanding of best practices for library management. Engaging in these opportunities not only enhances individual skills but also contributes to the collective advancement of the open-source ecosystem.

www.ingramcontent.com/pod-product-compliance
Lightning Source LLC
Chambersburg PA
CBHW070946050326
40689CB00014B/3363

* 9 7 9 8 3 1 4 4 3 6 2 8 8 *